THE BEAUTY IN OUR BROKENNESS

RAGAN SARTIN

authorHOUSE®

AuthorHouse™
1663 Liberty Drive
Bloomington, IN 47403
www.authorhouse.com
Phone: 1 (800) 839-8640

Published by AuthorHouse 06/29/2019

ISBN: 978-1-7283-1778-6 (sc)
ISBN: 978-1-7283-1794-6 (e)

Print information available on the last page.

Scripture taken from The Holy Bible, King James Version. Public Domain

DEDICATION

For my Heavenly Father who created me, who loves me and who is the ultimate Author of this book. May You receive all the glory, honor and praise.

CONTENTS

ACKNOWLEDGEMENTS

From Ragan,

First and foremost I want to acknowledge my Heavenly Father and my Lord and Savior Jesus Christ. Just as You told the prophet Jeremiah, I know You knew me before You formed me in my mother's womb. Your hands fashioned me. You molded me and shaped me with a perfect plan and purpose in mind.

My life was forever changed the day I first met You. That was the day I first acknowledged You and realized what You had done for me. I accepted You totally and completely as Savior and Lord of my life. That day in August of 2005, I tasted and seen that You are REALLY REAL and so SO good! Old things passed away that day and all things were made new. I became a new creation that day. That was the day I truly began to live!

If there is anything good in me Lord it is You. To You belongs ALL THE GLORY and ALL OF THE PRAISE! May my life be a living testimony to Your love, grace and power. May the world see You in me. May my shortcomings and failures point only to You as the One who forgives, heals and redeems.

Without You I can do nothing and I never want to try. With You all things are possible, so may I always walk by faith and not by sight, may I trust in You who spoke and it was so and may I never let go of the hand of the One who promised to never leave me nor forsake me.

I love you Lord.

To Joey:

Other than Jesus, You are my rock and the rock of our family. God knew what He was doing when He made you, and He made you just for me. You are my biggest supporter, my teammate, my go-to. You are my home. I don't think there is anything we can't do together, as long as I have the instruction manual and you have the tools. Our life together has been quite the ride so far and I can't wait to see what God has in store for our future. I love you.

Savanna and Caleb:

Two of God's greatest blessings to me. Nothing has taught me more, stretched and challenged me further or blessed me greater than being your mother. I didn't receive a handbook on the do's and don'ts, although I would have been the first in line for a copy of Motherhood for dummies. I know I have probably failed more than I have succeeded, but your best is something I've always strived to give and provide.

My prayer for you both is first and foremost that you have a personal relationship with the One who loves you more than I, or anyone else ever could. I pray that you both live your lives fully devoted to the One who gave it and that you live the life God uniquely created you for. I pray you stay in the center of God's will and that when you fail-you get back up and never give up! I pray that you never settle for less than God's best for your lives and that no matter what, you always know you are loved with ALL OF MY HEART. You both are my GREATEST MINISTRY.

Tavryn James:

My first grandbaby. Grandma's little man. When I found out about you, I began to pray for you. As we awaited your arrival, I knew God was knitting you together in your mommy's belly. So, I prayed that God would give you a heart that loved Him more than anything or anyone. I prayed that He would give you a servant's heart and one that would follow Him all the days of your life. I prayed that He would give you eyes to see as Jesus sees, hands that will reach out to the hurting and feet that will spread the gospel of Jesus Christ. It is my prayer that you serve God all the days of your life. Jeremiah 29:11. Love, Grandma

Mom:

Where do I start? You are the one who I have been with for the longest. I know what your heart sounds like from the inside and I know what it looks *like on the outside. There is no other person in this world that has a heart like yours. You are the most selfless human being I have ever known. You have spent my entire life giving your all to everyone around you. Your example has influenced my life and has helped shape me into who I am today. We have experience a lot in our relationship as mother and daughter and I believe the greatest realization is that God is truly a restorer of the broken. My prayer is that you know that you are loved more than you know and that you have made an eternal difference in my life just by being you. LOVE YOU!*

To my bubby (Phillip):

You were my first go-to. I could always depend on you to be there for me-whether it was to defend me or to pick me up when I fell (except for that one time when you secretly pushed me face first into that muddy ditch-sorry David for the spankin'). Being your sister has been quite the adventure. I am so thankful for all of the memories we share. No matter what I'm always here for you. Your sissy

To all my family:

God in His wisdom, wonderfully and uniquely designed the family unit. Oh, the creation He made when He put all of us together! Each one of us are different in our interests, our pursuits and in the direction we have went in our lives-yet we are all linked by one common bond-the bond of family. Each one of you have made a difference in my life and helped shape me into who I am today. My prayer for my entire family is that every single one of us come to a saving knowledge of Jesus Christ so that when this life is over, our family circle will remain unbroken. May God raise up a mighty army for His Kingdom in my family! I love you all!

To my best friends Alex and Missy Harrison:

There is no doubt in my mind that God divinely connected my life with yours! You both have been a God send to Joey and I. The spiritual realities that you have imparted into our lives are priceless and continue to impact our lives and marriage. Your greatest impact continues to be not what you've said but what you've lived. Your lives have truly been an example from the very beginning. *I am so thankful for our friendship and all of the memories we share. Throughout the years working together in ministry we have been through a lot but I can truly say there have been more ups than downs, more victories than losses and more laughter than tears. It has been one of the greatest joys of my life. May we never get tired of our float trips-no matter how much tackle we lose and may our friendship leads us all the way to the river of life and we can sort it all out there! Love you both!*

A special thanks to all of you who have supported me, prayed for me and stood with me. I wouldn't be here today without all of you and this book certainly would not have been possible without you. Thank you to the special one who obeyed God and called me making this book a _literal_ possibility. Thank you to my church family, I love you all- you are THE BEST!

Thank you to Kyla Bowers for hooking me up with Shane Farmer who helped me tremendously in this process! Thank you so much for your time and expertise Shane, I really appreciate all of your time and help!

Thank you to Tammy Morton for photographing the picture for my cover-I love it. Thank you to Autumn Maggard for our family photos-you are awesome! Thank you to Lacey Moore for your time and coming out to take my author photo for me, I appreciate you!

Thank you to Dustin Davis at Authorhouse for your patience, and for your persistence, I appreciate all of your help!

Thank you to each and every one of you. There is not enough time, or paper space to include every name that should be written, so please know that if you know me then know that _you_ have made a difference in my life-so thank _YOU_! GOD BLESS EACH AND ALL!

INTRODUCTION

It is human nature to want to avoid pain, but no one escapes it. Billions of dollars are spent each year in the pursuit of making our pain non-existent, and at the minimum-bearable. If you will take a look at the pharmaceutical companies of today, you will see exactly what I am talking about-there is virtually a pill for anything that ails you. The fact of life is that we have all experienced our fair share of pain, yet that doesn't make us "used" to it- nor does it make us want to experience it again. But pain is inevitable no matter who you are. Pain is not biased and it knows no bounds. It doesn't matter who you are, or where you are from. It doesn't matter whether you are rich or poor, tall or short. Everyone experiences pain-physically and emotionally.

Jesus came to this earth and took our suffering upon Himself. Isaiah 53:5 KJV says ***"But He was wounded for our transgressions, He was bruised for our iniquities: the chastisement of our peace was upon Him; and with His stripes we ARE healed."*** Jesus was wounded for us. Jesus was bruised for us. Jesus was chastised for us. Jesus took stripes upon His body for our healing. Why then do we still suffer and experience pain? Why do Jesus loving people still get cancer? Why do they *die* from cancer? Why is there so much pain and brokenness in this world? There are many people have asked the same question: "If God is such a loving God, then why does He allow all of these things to happen?" I know that is a question that many have had and if I am guessing, many more have thought it but never dared to actually ask it out loud. But if you are honest, you probably have at least wondered that very same thing at least once in your life.

I can say that I do know that God IS a loving God but that doesn't mean that we will never experience pain and suffering- even loss. There are some things we don't understand, and *won't* understand down here.

There are so many things that we experience in this life that we just don't know the answer to. But one thing that I am sure of is that God knows all things and He has a greater plan, and one that is many times so far above our current understanding here on earth. I believe that there are times that we can have the wrong **perspective** on pain, on struggles and hardships, and on the trials and even *tragedies* that happen in our lives. We definitely don't like any of these things, but I think we have missed the beauty in all of it. Did I say BEAUTY? Yes, Beauty. There is beauty because I believe there is much greater PURPOSE in our pain, a PLAN in our hardships, and TRIUMPH in every trial and tragedy in our lives.

> Isaiah 61:1-3 KJV says *"The Spirit of the Lord God is upon me; because the Lord hath anointed me to preach good tidings unto the meek; he hath sent me to bind up the brokenhearted, to proclaim liberty to the captives, and the opening of the prison to them that are bound: to proclaim the acceptable year of the Lord, and the day of vengeance of our God; to comfort all that mourn; To appoint unto them that mourn in Zion, to give unto them beauty for ashes, the oil of joy for mourning, the garment of praise for the spirit of heaviness; that they might be called trees of righteousness, the planting of the Lord, that He might be glorified."*

"That He might be glorified." Did you catch that? Do we think that the only way for God to get glory out of our lives is when everything in our life is going wonderful? Sure He gets glory when His blessings are being poured out into our families, our relationships and our finances. But how does God get glory out of the ash heap? How does He get the glory in our times of loss and despair? How does God get glory when we feel like our situation is more than we can bear? These are the times in our lives that we would much rather bypass and avoid completely, but it's in these difficult times when God gets the **most** glory! How? Because when we are weak-He shows Himself to be strong. When we feel like our situation is impossible and impassable; He makes a way where there seems to be no way-every single time!

It's all of the precious lessons that we learn *in* and *through* the pain, the struggles, the hardships and the tragedies that we can truly say there is beauty or glory to be had! In and through all of the difficult seasons in life we learn that God is God. We learn that He really does love us! In suffering, we learn a depth of the love of God like we never knew at any other time in our life. When we have nothing else to hold onto or no-one else to turn to but God, we find out that He is everything we need! We learn that He doesn't leave us in our hard times but that He is with us and that He does bring us through it all.

God has been tested and has been proven true! Just open His word and read about Job. Job was a man of God. Job loved God and served God, yet we read how he suffered greatly and beyond anything we can imagine. But Job never gave up and he held on to God through it all. Job trusted in God's faithfulness and God proved to be faithful to Job. We read in Job 42:12 KJV: *"So the Lord blessed the latter end of Job more than his beginning..."* Read on and you will see that the Lord gave Job DOUBLE of everything that he had lost! "Double for his trouble." God brought compete restoration in Job's life; I don't know about you, but that gives *me* hope let me tell ya!

Life is a journey. It has many rugged mountains, deep and dark valleys, gentle slopes and crazy crooked turns! Looking back, no matter what I have ever faced, Jesus Christ has been the one and only constant. When the storms of life came crashing in, and the winds and waves of trial beat upon my life, I was able to make it through every single storm because my life is built upon that solid foundation-which is Jesus Christ the Lord! Through different circumstances of life, I have suffered heartbreak, devastation and even loss; after all, Jesus said in this world we WOULD have tribulation. But even so, I can truly say that I have been able to find the beauty in my brokenness! I may not know what tomorrow will bring, but I know who does. I am putting my trust in the One who has taken my messes and made a message, my tests and made testimonies and taken every trial and caused me to triumph in every single one of them!

Follow along with me as I share with you my journey of writing this very book. There are struggles no doubt that I will encounter. Trials will surely come my way. Pain is inevitable, but there is one thing that will no doubt accompany this journey: the presence and the power of God. Here goes my first step of my journey...may God receive ALL OF THE GLORY!

CHAPTER 1

JUST DO IT!

January 1, 2017 was the beginning of a new year-a new start. Isn't that what everyone says in the New Year? We all know about new year's resolutions don't we? Anything from losing weight to spending less money, we all want to do better and to be better. For me, 2017 wasn't about a resolution but a decision-a decision to act. Prior to the new year2017 came a day that became a *defining moment* in my life, and one that would shape not only the new year, but every day of my life- from that day forward.

It was late December, the year 2016 was coming to a close and I had no idea that my whole perspective was about to change. It was just after Christmas, and my husband had returned to work, leaving our son and I to enjoy what was left of his Christmas break. We woke up that morning to an average December morning-dreary and cold. Just across the highway from our house, there is an old missionary Baptist church. I glanced out the window and noticed a hearse parked next to the front door. I knew why they were there. The mother of a friend of mine had passed away just a couple of days prior and this was the day of her funeral. The hearse was the first to arrive. I went about our morning as usual, and I found myself taking an occasional glance out of the window to see if anyone else had arrived. It was still early, so no one had made it yet, but I noticed that the back door of the hearse stood open, and there sat the casket. The funeral directors were inside the church and there the casket sat- staring toward our house. I had never gotten the chance to meet my friend's mother, but I was sure my friend was heartbroken. As I looked at the casket sitting in the back of the car, I couldn't help but wonder about her. I didn't know if she knew the Lord, or if she lived for Him, but I remember thinking that if she did serve God, whatever she did for Him in this life was over. That startling realization that I had as I looked out my window that day made me look at my own life. I wondered, *'if I should pass away soon, have I done all that I want to do for God?'* My answer and realization about my own life was *'NO I haven't!'* And then my next thought was- WHAT am I waiting for? *WHO* am I waiting for? I have things in my heart that I want to do for God and I have never acted on them. I have a God-given vision to be a servant of the Lord and do the work He has called me to do. God has placed gifts in me, and He wants me to use what He has given me. Right then and there, as I pondered all of these things, I made more than a new year's resolution; I made a DECISION to "Just Do It". It is more than a resolution-it is a life change. I decided that day that whatever God has put in my heart to do-*Just Do It!* That became what I call my "motto" for 2017: JUST DO IT…So I am! I am stepping out and putting action behind the vision. I am putting feet to my faith. I am going to be a doer of the word that God has put in my heart. You are holding a piece of my vision in your hands right now! This is my first book. I always knew I would write a book and that I would "just know" when it was time. Well, this is the book and the time is now. I am going to JUST DO IT!

So let me ask you-what or who is holding **you** back from doing what God has placed in your heart? Many times we discover that it's not so much *what* is holding us back, as it is *who* is holding us back, and many times the who is us! So much of the time we can be our own worst enemy. We don't need any more critics because we do a bang up job at being our own. So, ask yourself why. Why is it that you aren't stepping up to the plate? Why is God's calling on your life unanswered? Is it fear-the fear of failure? Is it because you feel like you don't "know enough"? Maybe it's just that you feel you are absolutely *unqualified* to do that *thing* the Lord has put in your heart. Let me tell you that whatever **it** is that is holding you back is the very thing that is keeping you from living your fullest potential! That internal dialog that you keep hidden safely in the depths of your mind is holding you and your God-given destiny hostage! Don't let fear define your life! Don't let anything stop you from just doing that thing that God has put inside you! You just might be "unqualified" in terms of man's conditions and requirements, but that's ok, because it is God who qualifies you-not man! <u>If God has called you, God has qualified you!</u> Are you hesitant to step out of your comfort zone and into the unknown? Do not let fear paralyze you. Step out in faith and watch what God will do. God will honor your obedience and your step of faith!

Consider adopting my motto for 2017: Just Do it, and whatever you want to do for God... JUST DO IT! Don't let the fear of failure stop you! Remember Peter? He stepped out, and he also began to sink, but the Lord didn't let him sink all the way-he *began* to sink. Peter cried out to Jesus and immediately Jesus lifted him up from the waves. He began to sink, not because he could not walk to Jesus on the water, but because he took his eyes off of the Lord and looked at the obstacles around him. Don't look at all of the obstacles that may be standing in between you and your God given destiny. Look past the obstacles to the One who calls you out on the water. Take the step. Just Do It!

CHAPTER 2

BLESSED ASSURANCE

My life has had many ups and downs, mountains and valleys. There have been times when I felt the presence and the power of God so strong and there have been times I had to walk by faith-trusting His word that tells me that He never leaves me nor forsakes me. 2016 proved to be a "walking by faith" year for me.

The year 2016 started out with the same enthusiasm that I usually have when it comes to a new year. I begin every year seeking the Lord in prayer as to what kind of goal He would have for me for that year. I felt that 2016 was to be a "get out of your comfort zone" kind of year. I was reminded of Peter when he saw Jesus coming to them on the sea-walking on the water. Peter definitely got out of his comfort zone when he asked the Lord to bid him to come on the water, and so Jesus did! Peter stepped right out of the boat and on the water. We all know what happened next, but Peter was brave enough to take that chance! He may have sunk, but not completely- the Lord rescued him! Peter often gets a bad rap, but there's one thing about him in this particular situation-Peter didn't have to live with a "What if". This was the beginning of a brand new year for me, and suddenly, I knew the Lord was challenging me to trust Him and do what I had never done before, but I had no idea how far out of my comfort zone I would actually get.

January 2016 came and went, and by February things began to change in my life. I had finally decided it was time to go to the doctor and get some things checked out-things that I had put off for way too long. So,

I went to my OB/GYN and had the routine tests done. In the exam the nurse noticed something that wasn't right. She immediately performed a biopsy on a mass that she discovered on my cervix, and told my husband and I that she was almost positive that it was cancer. She couldn't give us a definitive answer that day, so we were sent home to wait for the results of the biopsy. In the meantime, our best friend Alex Harrison, (who is also our Pastor), began talking about his need for an Assistant Pastor, and that I was the one that he had in mind for the position. By the first of March the congregation appointed me as the Assistant Pastor of our church. I accepted the position with excitement and with great reverence to the Lord for the responsibilities in which I was now entrusted. My excitement grew as I stepped into this new walk with the Lord. Everything seemed to be going wonderful as far as ministry was concerned and then we got the call. It was that one phone call that changes your life. The call that defines a journey. The nurse informed me that my biopsy results were in and the doctor wanted to see me immediately. I could tell by the tone in her voice that it was serious. She told me that she could not discuss the results over the phone, so right then and there I knew it probably wasn't good news. We were scheduled an appointment the following day. My husband and I sat in the office and received the news that no one wants to hear: *"You have cancer."* I have heard different stories of how people reacted to the same kind of news but I'm sure my reaction was not the typical response the Doctor was expecting that I would have; I actually surprised myself. After I received that news, I had a deep sense of peace sweep over me, and I KNEW that I was going to be okay. My husband and I were asked repeatedly: "Are you ok?" and our response was the same: *"yes."* I explained to the doctor that I had faith in God and that I knew I would be okay *no matter what.* The doctor was not convinced, so she sent in a 'Behavioral Health Consultant', to make sure we were okay. As she entered the room, she met us with sympathy and the same concern that my doctor had: *"Are you sure you're ok?"* she asked, with a look of devastation written all over her face. We reassured her over and over that we were definitely okay. So realizing we were not in need of her services, she left-but not before giving me her card and an offer to call her anytime, *"in case you change your mind and need someone to talk to."* she said. I was grateful for their care and concern for me, but it was if they were more concerned about my situation than I was. It seemed that they could not understand how someone could be okay knowing they had cancer. I'm not saying we weren't initially scared, or shocked when we heard the news. We had our moment. But I had an even greater sense of peace to come over me and I knew that it was the peace of God. I was assured that no matter what I had to face, God was with me and I was going to be okay no matter what happened. God gave me that *"Blessed Assurance."*

In the age-old hymn *Amazing Grace*, there is a verse that states: *"Through many dangers, toils and snares I have already come, 'tis grace hath brought me safe thus far and grace will lead me home."* I can say Amen more than a few times to that verse! I truly believe that the peace that I had in the beginning of my journey with cancer was because of the things in my life that the Lord had already brought me through. Dangers, toils and snares had been many up and to that point, but God's grace had brought me safe through them all, and I just knew that cancer was not going to be any different. Whether that meant God would bring me through safely to the other side and I would be with Him, or this was another trial that He would see me safely through and I would have another testimony to share on this earth I wasn't sure-but like Paul I was sure that to live is Christ and to die is gain-either way I was a winner.

Many tests, and scans and blood work followed my cancer diagnosis that day. I was immediately referred to a gynecological oncologist to do my follow up care. I met with him, had my exam and we discussed my options. I chose to have a radical hysterectomy which would also remove the 5 cm. tumor that was on my cervix. On May 3, 2016 I underwent the surgery. I had no idea the pain and recovery of such a surgery. Up and to this point, the only surgery I had was when my tonsils were removed when I was 13. I never had any pain to speak of other than normal and I hadn't had any major health issues until this. The pain was beyond what I could have imagined. I woke up after surgery-still in the operating room. The pain was so extreme, that I prayed out loud to God to take away the pain or take me out of this world. I prayed to die, **literally**

God sees what we can't and He understands what we don't

and I meant every word of it. Looking back, I can tell you that God *did not* take away my pain. He made it bearable. Obviously, He didn't answer my prayer to take me out of this world either. <u>God sees what we can't and He understands what we don't</u>. There are many times that we don't understand what is happening in our lives. We pray for a specific thing to happen, and when God doesn't give us the answer we think we need, we begin to question why. When we have waited and waited on God for an answer to come, and we haven't received answer, we wonder if He really does love us. But God does love us. He loves us *so much*, and that is why He answers our prayers-not with the answer that we think is right, or in the time frame that we think He should, but He answers with the best answer in the perfect time. I can look back in my life at some of the prayers I have prayed. At the time, I thought I knew what was best. I EARNESTLY prayed and petitioned God with my request. But today, I thank God for UNANSWERED PRAYER! I see now that at times, if God had given me some of the things I thought I needed, it would have been a disaster. The whole course of my life would have been changed. In the middle of life's toughest battles, when situations seemed hopeless and when pain was the only thing I could feel, those were the times I had forgotten <u>God knows best</u>. He sees ahead. He knows the beginning and He knows the end and everything in between. I am reminded of Psalmist David. In Psalm 139:1-6 KJV: *"O Lord, thou hast searched me, and known me. Thou knowest my downsitting and mine uprising, thou understandest my thought afar off. Thou compassest my path and my lying down, and art aquainted with all my ways. For there is not a word in my tongue, but, lo, O LORD, thou knowest it altogether. Thou hast beset me behind and before, and laid thine hand upon me. Such knowledge is too wonderful for me; it is high, I cannot attain unto it."* God knows. God sees and yes-God has the best answer.

I am so inspired by the story of the great Corrie Ten Boom, survivor of the Holocaust. She experienced unbelievable horror and loss; yet through it all, she didn't give up. By the grace of God and her faith IN GOD, she made it out of the concentration camps, and went on to do a mighty work for the kingdom of God. There is a poem that is called "Life is but the weaving" which is sometimes attributed to her, and understandably so, but actually, the author is unknown. It is one of my favorite poems, as it speaks volumes to me and I'd like to share some of it with you:

"Life is but the weaving"

My life is but a weaving
Between my God and me.
I cannot choose the colors
He weaveth steadily.
Oft' times He weaveth sorrow;
And I in foolish pride
Forget He sees the upper
And I the underside

One of my favorite lines in that poem is: *"And I in foolish pride, forget He sees the upper and I the underside."* There are many times in life, we tend to forget how limited our understanding is, especially in contrast to God and **why** He has allowed us to go through some of the things that we face. One thing we learn during the hardest, most trying times in our lives is that God is God. His wisdom and understanding is unsearchable. Isaiah 40:28 KJV the Lord Himself asked **"Hast thou not known? Hast thou not heard, that the everlasting God, the Lord, the Creator of the ends of the earth, fainteth not, neither is weary? There is no searching of His understanding."** The Apostle Paul was well aware of God's unsearchable wisdom and knowledge as he wrote these words to the church in Rome: **"O the depth of the riches both of the wisdom and knowledge of God! How unsearchable are His judgments, and His ways past finding out! For who hath known the mind of the Lord? Or who hath been His counselor? Or who hath first given to Him, and is shall be recompensed unto Him again? For of Him, and through Him, and to Him, are all things: to whom be glory for ever. Amen."** (Romans 11:33-36 KJV). God's wisdom is so far above and beyond our own, it is not limited and it can never be exhausted! God was well aware of the beginning of our lives, when we took our very first breath, and only He knows the day when we will take our last. God also knows every moment of every day in between. With all of the understanding that we do have, we still have no way of knowing what the ending of our day will be, let alone the next 5 minutes! Only when we are able to look back over our lives are we able to see things more clearly and get a better understanding of the big picture. Take a hiker for instance. When the hiker has made it to the top of the mountain, he/she is able to get a view of the whole landscape. Only when they are standing on the top of the mountain are they able to see more clearly the steps it took for them to get to the top! They are also standing at the best vantage point possible to devise the safest route back down that mountain! The view from the mountaintop is very different from the steps up that rocky slope. By standing on the top of the mountain, they have gained a much different perspective- and so it is in our journey with the Lord. You may be in the heat of the battle right now. Like that hiker, you are climbing a mountain; maybe the biggest you have ever faced. It may very well feel like Mt. Everest to you at the moment. You are hot and tired. You wonder how much further until you reach the top. You wonder if you have the strength to keep climbing. It is at this point that you need to stop a moment and catch your breath. Reevaluate your steps. Take a minute to get the right perspective about your situation. Don't look at how far you have to go, just take one step at a time. Keep putting one foot in front of the other. Remember that although you may feel like you are on this journey by yourself, you are not traveling alone-God is with you. In the moments you feel like you can't go on, call upon the Lord. He is there to help you. When you feel you're at your lowest, remember God is with you and He will bring you through it!

There have been many things that I have faced in my life that I didn't understand, but I have learned that God has a plan, and not just *a* plan but the very ***best*** plan. He only gives us what is best. In the case of me praying to die after my surgery, if God did give me what I wanted at the time, I wouldn't be here now to write this book. If God had granted me that sincere request, I wouldn't have seen how God caused me to overcome it all. I wouldn't be here to tell you that being a born-again child of God doesn't make us exempt from pain and suffering, but I can tell you that even so, there is HOPE! I am able to tell you there is a stronger version of you on the other side of your difficulty if you will not give up or give in! I can say that whatever you may be going through-God is there! You may not feel Him, but He said He would never leave you or forsake you!

I am here today to tell you that God brought me through everything! I am able to tell you that God will use everything for the good! That is the understanding that I have received hindsight. That is the perspective I have gained standing from the top of my mountain.

There is a facade in the world that portrays that because we are Christians, that means our lives are problem free and that we live on the "mountaintop" every single day. I'm sorry honey, but I'll be the first to tell you that the Christian walk is not a mountaintop to mountaintop experience. That is impossible. You must go through the valley to get to the mountain, and you must climb the mountain to get to the mountaintop! Our journey will be filled with mountaintop experiences, and thank God for that, but our journey will also be filled with valley walking. Walking in the "valley" is a bittersweet journey. It is a very trying time. It means completely walking by faith. It is where you learn that dying to your flesh and walking after the Spirit is an absolute requirement in order to make it through it. This spiritual valley experience can be a very lonely time-sometimes the loneliest. But, the valley is also a very fruitful time for us to grow spiritually. Have you ever realized, naturally speaking, that there's not a whole lot that grows on the mountaintop? It is in the valley where the richest resources are found that supplies the sustenance for growth and life-and so it is spiritually! It is in the valley that we find out that the life-sustaining truths such as, how the Lord never leaves us-even in our most difficult and hard to understand moments; He truly is a friend that sticks closer than any brother. It is in the valley that we cling to Him tighter, and His faithfulness is proven true. In my valley experience of walking through all of the physical and emotional pain that came with my journey with cancer, I was affected spiritually as well. Anyone who has ever been sick knows the discouragement you face. It was when I was in the "heat of the battle" that I was the most vulnerable to those feelings of discouragement, hopelessness and thoughts of down-right giving up and throwing in the towel-not on God but on myself. At the time, my valley experience didn't feel very fruitful! The struggles and the trials felt very overwhelming at times: <u>But God</u>. Those are two words that I am so thankful for...BUT GOD. It takes time for fruit to grow, and it took time for me to see the reasons behind my valley experience, and a little longer to see the fruit in my life that was produced because of it. He brought me through my valley.

He brought me through it all. All of the moments I felt like staying in bed with a blanket pulled up over my head, all of the moments that I was angry because it felt like no one really cared what I was going through, and all of the moments where it felt like I was completely swallowed up in the dark clouds of discouragement. At the time, I didn't feel like I could make it, **but God** carried me through it. I didn't give up; I kept putting one foot in front of the other. In the moments that I could not go on, the Lord carried me. Now, as I stand on the mountain looking out at where I have been, I can tell you that I would never trade one of those steps in my journey. It was those very steps that brought me to the place I stand today. I finally have a different perspective because now I am standing where I have a better view. I can finally see now, that I am stronger than I was before the journey, and that the journey was necessary for my growth! Now I am able to say I am so thankful! I want to tell you that no matter what you have to face in life; God will bring you through it all! King David experienced a valley experience, and he shared his thoughts in the book of Psalm. Chapter 23 of the book of Psalms is one of the most quoted chapters of the Bible, and especially at funerals because it brings so much comfort as we are facing loss. Personally, I think it would do ourselves so much good if we took this Psalm to heart and applied it to our own situations while we are alive. Consider where David's comfort came from as he walked through his valley experience. *"Yea, though I walk through the valley of the shadow of death, I will fear no evil: for thou art with me; thy rod and thy staff they comfort me."* (Psalm 23:4 KJV) The key to David's strength in the valley was that he knew that he was not alone, God was with him! It is such a comfort to know that our Heavenly Father walks with us! David acknowledged the fact that yes; he was walking through a valley. David was not walking through just any valley, but he described it as the *"valley of the shadow of death"* (Psalm 23:4KJV) It was a very trying time in David's life! Just as David walked through that valley, the three Hebrew children walked in the midst of a burning fiery furnace. They were able to make it through it all because they were not alone, the Lord was with them! No matter where you are in your journey, you are going to make it through! You may not understand the what's and the whys or even the how's, but don't ever give up! GOD WILL BRING YOU THROUGH IT ALL! Right now you may be walking in what looks and feels like the valley of the shadow of death, but know that just like King David, God is with you and your mountaintop awaits!

Psalm 102:19-28 KJV: "For He hath looked down from the height of His sanctuary; from heaven did the Lord behold the earth; to hear the groaning of the prisoner; to loose those that are appointed to death; To declare the name of the Lord in Zion, and His praise in Jerusalem; When the people are gathered together, and the kingdoms, to serve the Lord. He weakened my strength in the way; He shortened my days: thy years are throughout all generations. Of old hast thou laid the foundation of the earth: and the heavens are the work of thy hands. They shall perish, but thou shalt endure: yea, all of them shall wax old like a garment; as a vesture shalt thou change them, and they shall be changed: But thou art the same, and thy years shall have no end. The children of thy servants shall continue, and their seed shall be established before thee."

CHAPTER 3

GOD IS WORKING A WORK

Don't you just love the many ways that the Lord will speak to you sometimes? He speaks to me through everyday things…a storm damaged tree, a beautiful butterfly or a breathtaking sunrise or sunset-things that we are used to seeing everyday and often take for granted. Only God can use these things to touch the deepest places in your spirit.

Just the other day, the Lord did just that. I had been in the house for longer than I had liked. It is January, so you will get my point when I say I had a little bit of *cabin fever.* On this particular day, the sun had finally decided to shine, so I was really drawn to go outside and soak up some of that gorgeous sunshine. I was looking forward to feeling the rays on my skin. I had my morning coffee and devotions with the Lord and got dressed to go out and enjoy the outdoors for awhile. As I got dressed, I was anticipating enjoying some communion with the Lord. I had been fervently seeking the Lord once again on whether I should do what the doctor has strongly recommended, and that is to do the follow up treatment to my surgery, which is chemotherapy and radiation. On my last two appointments I have refused the treatment. During my most recent appointment on January 12, my thoughts regarding me taking the treatment are beginning to change. They are concerned with some of the symptoms I am having, and they are urgently recommending chemo and radiation again. They have ordered a CT scan to check to see if the cancer is back or has spread, but regardless of the results-they want to do the treatments. I was told that it is not IF the cancer will come back, but

WHEN and WHERE. So, on this particular day, I had been back on my knees regarding this decision. I had prayed and prayed, but I hadn't got the answer on what I should do. I was *waiting* and *wanting* the Lord to tell me: *"This is the way, walk ye in it"*, but the answer hadn't come. I was pleading with the Lord, but nothing.

On this day, I finally decided to quit *begging* God for an answer and just wait for God *to* answer. I went to the Lord, and told Him that I knew that *He knew* that I needed direction and that I was waiting on Him to guide me. And not only waiting for Him to show me what to do, but that I was in a position to hear Him when He spoke. I was in a position of expectancy. That day, I felt a release because I finally released my frustration for the answer and put my trust and focus on the Lord. I knew my answer would come when He wanted me to know it, and until then, I was just going to wait it out and keep on living life and doing the things that I do. I was excited to get outside and get a breath of fresh air and just enjoy the sunshine and the presence of the Lord.

When I stepped out of my door, the sun was shining, but I wasn't met with the warmth on my skin that I had imagined, but a very cold wind on my face. It was the kind of cold and wind that when you feel it, it pierces to the bone and you automatically want to run into any place that has heat-in my case it was my house. But, I didn't turn around and go back in my house because the Lord automatically began to talk to me. He showed me that just like my reaction was to run back into my house where the heat was and avoid the cold and the wind is exactly what we do when it comes to pain, trials and hardships in our lives. We don't want any kind of pain. We don't want trials, and we definitely don't want hardship of any kind; and honestly, who does? We want to avoid pain. We like it when everything is going good-when the bills are all paid, and there is money left in the bank... when our kids are excelling in life...when we are getting the promotions, the pay raises and the bonuses at work. We would much rather bypass the hard stuff. We would much rather go through life and never have to experience trouble of any kind. We all know that is not reality, but oh how we wish it was! Difficulty in life comes in many different forms, but when difficulty does hit our home, we want to get through it the fastest way possible. We want to take the path of least resistance.

COUNTING IT ALL JOY

Many of us are familiar with the scripture in James 1: 2 KJV that says ***"My brethren, count it all joy when ye fall into divers temptations."*** Countless church congregations throughout history have heard this scripture quoted and many chuckles have come from the pews of those congregations, as we wonder just what James was thinking when he told us to "count it all joy." Is He insane? It seems as if James is living on a different planet. Some have said: "Count it all joy huh? Well he must not have had to deal with kids like I have." The one thing we miss as we are trying to figure out just how we are to "count it all joy" is the rest of that scripture - which holds our answer. James isn't insane, and he wasn't living on another planet. James went on to tell us *how* we "count it all joy." Read past verse 2 and read verses 3 and 4- ***"<u>Knowing this</u>, that the trying of your faith worketh patience. But let patience have her perfect work, that ye may be perfect and entire, wanting nothing."*** (KJV) There it is. There is our answer. How do we "*count it all joy*"? The scripture says, KNOWING THIS. Knowing what? ***"<u>That the trying of your faith worketh patience</u>"***. Do you know that God uses every pain, every trial and every hardship in our lives for a greater purpose? None of it is in vain! It says *"That the trying of your faith worketh patience."* When we understand what James is telling us in this scripture, we will be able to understand how God causes good to come out of some of the worst circumstances in our lives. Let's look at the words *trying, worketh* and *patience*.

Let's start with the word "trying". What comes to mind when you read that word? Many of us tend to think of temptations when we read that word. We think of the temptations that entice us and try to draw us away and pull us from our faith. That is not what this word means. The word 'trying' means: *"proving" or "to prove"*. Our faith has to be <u>proven</u>. The only way to "prove" the genuineness of our faith is to put it to the test. Remember when you were in grade school? When we look back through our school years, we can remember that each day our teacher had a lesson for us. We were always learning new things. However, before the teacher taught us a new subject, she gave us a test to see what we had already learned. She had to see whether or not we had the knowledge and understanding of the things she had been teaching us in her lessons. Our knowledge and understanding was put to the test.

TESTED FAITH

One way our faith is proven is by "obstacles" that come our way in life. Anyone can serve God when everything is going great in life, but what about when life isn't going great at all? Do we still serve Him with the same enthusiasm when things are not so great? Do we still have the same trust in God when things seem to be falling apart? Do we run away from God or do we run to Him during these times? When we are in church we can raise our hands and shout hallelujah when we are with our brothers and sister in Christ, but do we still do the same after we walk out of the church and we face difficulties that no one sees? Do we still have praise on our lips when we are discouraged? What about when we are sick and hurting, how does one have praise then? We all have experienced these times, and while it may seem impossible to make it through, we must remember that with God all things are possible! Remember Job? Job showed us-it is possible. Job said in Job 13:15 KJV ***"Though He slay me, yet will I trust Him..."*** Job knew that he could trust in God. Even if he died, Job knew God had a plan. We must remember, that the genuineness of our faith must be proven and that is only done when we have nothing or no one else to hold on to but our faith in God.

THE END RESULT

The next two words we come to is "worketh patience". ***"The trying of your faith WORKETH PATIENCE."*** (James 1:3 KJV) The word *worketh* indicates accomplishment-to achieve a certain end result. God uses the situations in our lives that challenge us, and it's the challenge in itself that produces in us patience. Patience is the end result that God wants for every believer. The word "patience" here means **endurance.** Some of us think of this word negatively. We hear *endure* and we tend to think of putting up with some situation we aren't comfortable in, or a person with whom we don't particularly like. We think we are "enduring" when we have to go to our in-laws for the holidays, or deal with that boss who is always on our back. While God definitely uses these life experiences to teach us valuable lessons and to help us grow, the word endurance means so much more! It's more than just the *pressure* you are experiencing in your life; it's what the pressure *produces*! The word endurance means "the ability to withstand hardship or adversity; the ability to sustain a prolonged stressful effort or activity; the fact or power of enduring an unpleasant or difficult process or situation without giving way." In this scripture, the word endurance comes from the Greek word *hupomoné or hypomon* which is a combination of the words *hypó* which means "under" and *mènō* which means "remain". Together, endurance means to "remain under". To REMAIN under the pressure of circumstance! To withstand the hardships of life and still remain-to still be able to stand; to endure. How important it is in our Christian walk to have endurance! *Pressure builds endurance.* Trials, pain and difficulties of every kind not only *test* our faith but allows a "pressure" in our lives that in turn produces the end result in us that God wants-endurance. God works in our lives through every situation and circumstance to produce in us an inner determination; a "never give up" kind of attitude.

No matter what hardship we face in life, it is in these times that we must remember: whether God authored it or allowed it-it is not meant to destroy us or hurt us. Romans 8:28 tells us *"And we know that __all things work together for good__ to them who love God, to them who are the called according to His purpose."* If you are a child of God, you can be sure that God works all things out for <u>your good</u> and for <u>His glory</u>! We like the "good and the glory" part, but many of us don't want to have to go through the struggle it takes to get to the glory. The Lord reminded me of an athlete. An athlete doesn't just wake up one day and he is athletic. Take a runner for instance. He may have the passion for running, but he doesn't just hop out of bed and run a 10k. It takes training. In order to accomplish his goal, it takes focus and determination. If he wants to run the race and win, he has to strengthen his body through rigorous exercise and a disciplined diet. After the proper training beforehand, he is prepared for the race. If he is successful, he will come home with the trophy or the medal. In our walk with the Lord, He wants us to have the "trophy" and the "medal". We also want the trophy and the medal, but we tend to want to skip the training. We want to enjoy running through the finish line and hearing the applause, but we want to skip the self discipline it takes. We hear *rigorous exercises*, and disciplined *diet* and we forget about the dream of crossing the finish line. There are no short-cuts to success if you want to be recognized as a true athlete and there are no short-cuts if we want to be a successful tried and true child of God equipped with the ability to endure.

In order to endure some of the things I have faced in my own life, I have had to realize, that no matter what difficulty that it is, God has a great purpose for it. I may not have understood why I was going through some of the things I was faced with, but I trusted in the Lord and He brought me through everything. Only when I was able to look back, was I able to see how God used those obstacles and seemingly impossible situations to strengthen me and to make me who I am today. I was diagnosed with cancer, but God didn't give me cancer-he allowed it. Remember Job? God didn't give Job the boils that covered his body, but He allowed satan to afflict Job. God was the one in control. He allowed satan only a certain amount of opportunity, but with that allowance, God also put a boundary in place when He told satan not to touch his life. The enemy meant to destroy Job and his relationship with God. But God knew Job would not fail. God took what the enemy meant for harm and turned it all around for the good! Job's faith was being proven and God was doing a work in his life. Job endured his time of testing, and in the end God gave Job double for his trouble. The Bible says that **"the Lord blessed the latter end of Job more than his beginning..."** (Job42:12 KJV) Let me remind you that the same God who brought Job through his trials is the same God who is working in me and you right now! It may seem you will not make it through what you are facing, but keep your eyes on God and He will give you the strength and endurance you need to make it through your circumstance!

The final result of our endurance through the testing and the working process is found in the latter end of James 1:4 KJV -**"that you may be perfect and entire, wanting nothing."** In short, God wants us to be mature and complete Christ followers, who are equipped with an unbreakable endurance to keep forging ahead. It's not an easy process, but it is a required training for every born again child of God. The growing up process can be painful. When I was young, I had terrible growing pains in both of my legs. It was agonizing. But in order to grow from a toddler to an adolescent, there was a process of growing that I had to do. God sees our potential. It is going to take hard work and determination. It is going to take for us to push through the pain and get to the good stuff that God has for us. There is an old saying "No pain-no gain", that is so true. Anything that is worth something is going to cost us. We may have to learn to quit our complaining about our situations and realize that before we have a testimony, we have to have a test. Before we have a message, we have to go through a mess. Remember the athlete. For the one who never gives up, but endures the struggles and submits himself to the training that is needed, in the end, will be the one who finishes his race. In your time of testing, remember to hold on to God! He will give you the strength that you need! God will not fail you. 2 Corinthians 12:9 NIV says: ***"But He said to me, My grace is sufficient for you, for my power is made perfect in weakness. Therefore I will boast all the more gladly about my weaknesses, so that Christ's power may rest on me."*** God's grace is enough to see you through your trials. Remember: whatever it is-it didn't come to stay, it came to pass. In the end, there is a stronger, more determined you waiting when you cross your "finish line".

CHAPTER 4

WILLING TO SUFFER?

As I stood outside that day, all of a sudden it didn't matter as much to me that the cold wind was blowing on my face, because the Lord was ministering so deeply to my spirit. As I began to think about all of the good that has come from all of my struggles and even tragedies, I began to realize how *priceless* those times were in my life. I would never had known that God makes a way where there seems to be no way if I hadn't been faced with a seemingly impossible situations and seen how God makes what seems impossible to me- possible. I would have never known the agape love of God that picks you up from the depths of despair and binds up a broken heart unless I had been laying flat on my face with a broken heart. I would have never known the healing power of God for myself, if I had not had the experience of giving birth to a premature baby and see God strengthen him each and every day until the day we brought him home. Today he is a happy and healthy 6 year old boy with no complications whatsoever. God is truly a miracle working God.

During my time outside with God that day, He presented me with a question that I am still pondering in my heart today. He asked me: "Are you willing to suffer for my sake?" The question took me by surprise. Am I willing to **suffer** for His sake? The one thing that has been my hearts' desire since the day I was born again is to be a vessel for the Lord-to be a servant of God. So, when it comes to doing His work, I am all in- sign me up. When the Lord asked me this question, however, I was not quick to give an answer because I felt the seriousness of the question. I know that

I am willing to *sacrifice* for the cause of Christ, but am I willing to *suffer* for the cause of Christ? There is a weight when I think of that word-*Suffer*.

Anything that is really worth something in life is going to come at a cost. Jesus paid the ultimate cost when He paid the payment for the world's sin as he died on the cross. Through His death, burial and resurrection, he guarantees salvation for anyone who will believe. He overcame death, hell and the grave! Every single thing that Jesus did for mankind came at a cost. Knowing He came to seek and to save that which was lost, and to destroy the works of the devil, Jesus willingly left the glory of heaven and came to this earth. What a cost! He willingly left the Fathers side to be a servant! He left the splendor and glory of heaven knowing that would be rejected and ridiculed, mocked and whipped; and yet He came! The soldiers didn't take Jesus life, Jesus willingly laid it down. Jesus said in John 10:17-18 KJV *"Therefore does my Father love Me, because I lay down My life, that I might take it again. No man takes it from me, but I lay it down myself. I have power to lay it down, and I have power to take it again. This commandment have I received of My Father."* Jesus knew His purpose on earth. And while He hung on the cross, can you imagine for one second the determination it took for Him to remain hanging on the cross, all the while knowing He had the power to come off of the cross? The strength it took, as the soldiers mocked Him, and challenged Him, saying *"You who will destroy the Temple, and build it in three days, save yourself. If you be the Son of God, come down from the cross."* Matthew 27:40 KJV. What a cost, but Jesus paid it! He could have indeed come off of the cross and saved himself, showing the mockers that He IS who He said- but then He would not have been able save us! He had to suffer and die for our sake! What a cost! What LOVE! God the Father *is* love, and God paid the ultimate cost when He sent His Son to this world. John 3:16 KJV says *"For God so loved the world that He gave His only begotten Son, that whosoever believeth in Him should not perish, but have everlasting life."* A sacrifice had to be made to pay the price for sin and redeem mankind. Jesus was and is the only worthy sacrifice. Because Jesus suffered and died, yet rose again, my sins are forgiven and I have a new life!

I am so thankful that He was willing!

"Are you willing to suffer for my sake?" As I stood outside in the cold air

pondering all of these things in my heart, I realized that through all of the things God was ministering to my heart-I was receiving my answer. I knew God was leading me to go ahead with the chemotherapy and radiation. My answer to the Lord was and is yes-although I know right now that I have no idea in what *ways* I will suffer, or how it will feel *to suffer*. All that I do know right now is that God will be with me and He will help me. I know that whatever I may have to face, God will use it for His glory! There will be PURPOSE in my pain, a PLAN in my hardships, and TRIUMPH in every trial that I will face.

I truly believe that before we can truly live for God, we must be willing to die for God. If God doesn't have 100% of us, He doesn't have any part of us. As I said earlier, I know I can sacrifice for God, but am I willing to suffer for Him? Suffering to me means it is going to cost me probably more than I have ever paid in my walk with the Lord thus far. It is going to cost me my will-for His will, even when I don't understand why He wills me to suffer for Him. I know that no matter what may come and go, He is a good, good Father and I am His child. He has nothing but the very best planned for me! I put my life in His hands.

This is a song that I wrote on October 11, 2016; I believe it is very fitting to include it here:

"There's nothing you can't do"

When life seems uncertain, and doubt fills my mind, I run to my Father-every time, and He whispers "I love you, my child understand that I'll never leave you-you're in the palm of my hand

Chorus*: Make me an instrument, Lord that you can use, I know before you can there's some things you must do- so when the fire gets hot and it feels I won't make it through; help to remind me Lord, there's nothing you can't do.*

Now you may be in the middle of a trial's hottest flames, just remember who is with you-He knows you by name. Jesus still is that fourth man, and He's up and walkin' around, my friend this trial cannot defeat you-for you are standing on holy ground.

CHAPTER 5

WHEN LIFE'S DISAPPOINTMENTS REAPPOINTS US TO GODS DIVINE APPOINTMENTS

We have all heard it said: "hindsight is 20/20", and many of us know that statement to be the absolute truth. We all know the perfect vision we have when we are able to look back and see the bigger picture. This morning I am thinking about how Gods ways and thoughts are so much higher than ours and His plans are better-SO much better than ours!

God tells us in Isaiah 55:9 KJV: *"For as the heavens are higher than the earth, so are my ways higher than your ways, and my thoughts than your thoughts."*

I can look back over my life and I am so thankful that Gods ways and thoughts are so much higher than mine! God knows what is best, and He always gives what is best-even when His best comes in a different package than what we had hoped for.

This morning as I was looking through Facebook, I came across some pictures that a friend of mine had posted that were taken from Homecoming last night. They were pictures of her daughter and her classmates; you could see the bond that they shared. As I looked through each picture of the girls that my daughter went to high school with, I am reminded that sometimes God has other plans for our lives.

I admit-I cry sometimes. When I see the pictures of a basketball game played, I wonder what it would be like to be the "sports mom", proudly sporting the team shirt and carpooling all of the loud and obnoxious teenagers to their game. When I see the photos of special moments like Homecoming; all of the girls dressing up and looking beautiful, I think of the moms who were able to go dress shopping for the perfect dress. I think of those very special mother/daughter moments. I see the bond that these girls share with one another, as they experience life together. I see all of this, and it's feels like I'm on the outside looking in, wondering what it would be like to live those moments…but I will never know.

It's in these times that I feel cheated-like the devil has stolen so many things from me and now these precious moments too? I always dreamed of the day that my daughter would walk across the stage and get her diploma in the gym of the school where she started Preschool. I had all of the pictures stored away in my memory that I was going to use for her part in the senior video. There was that one that would have really embarrassed her, but one that is so cute and-it's my favorite. She was about 4 years old and she had been playing dress up that day. She came out of her bedroom as proud as could be with an outfit on that totally clashed. She had on a purple and pink sequined hat, with a matching outfit, but RED tights! She was so proud, she felt like a little princess. She pulled out the bench from under the piano, and she climbed on top to show off her new outfit. I snapped the picture. That one was the one I had always planned on going on the senior video for everyone to see. All of the pictures I had planned for that day were all so special and sure to bring tears to my eyes! I played out that day so many times in my head. But there will be no graduation this year with the kids she started preschool with. Today, while they are driving to Saturday basketball practice, my daughter is at her apartment, an hour and a half away. While her classmates are hanging out and having fun just being teenagers, she is with her precious baby boy-being a mommy.

I know what it is like to be a young teen mom. I had my daughter after I had just turned 17. I had dropped out of high school at the beginning of my 10th grade year. I was young and naive. I was not married when I had her, and by the time she turned one year old, I was a single teenage mom. It was not something I had aspired to be, but that's where I found myself. I know the struggles financially, physically and mentally. It definitely wasn't easy. I wanted her to experience life as a teenager and young adult.

I wanted her to have the freedom to figure out what she wanted to be in life and be able to go after her dreams. I didn't want her to experience the heavy responsibilities that I had at such a young age. But that wasn't to be for us. As it turns out, the one thing that I didn't want to happen-did, and it has also turned out to be one of the biggest blessings in my life! I absolutely LOVE my grandson! I love seeing the love that my daughter has for her child. It is amazing to see her as she looks at him. I will never forget the moment that I seen her look at him for the first time after giving birth. It was the look of love-*pure love*. I could see that she was realizing that this baby is someone who will love her no matter what and that she will have forever and love the same way. It was an unexpected blessing in our lives to say the least!

Around the year 2014, my husband and I were going through a very rough time with her, and God spoke to me while I was doing dishes one day. He said: ***"Her life is not going to go as you have planned."*** I absolutely dreaded those words! I thought for sure we were doomed! I cringed as I thought of what disaster was going to come about in our future with her. Today, as I look back, I am able to see that God was not sending me prophesy for disaster but God was giving me GREAT NEWS of encouragement! What kind of "plans" did I have for her? The very best plans that a parent can have for their child! I mentioned the "dreams" that I had wanted to see her experience and for me to experience with her. To me, seeing her experience being a teenager-shopping for the perfect dress, going to Homecoming, being the "sports mom" and watching her get her diploma is how I defined her success. But what God has shown me now and that He was trying to tell me 2 years ago is that her life is not going to go as I have planned but it is going to go as HE has planned!!! Gods plan for her life is her success. I know that HIS plan is the very best plan of all! My plans as her mother are very good, but her Heavenly Fathers plans are so much better! His plans are the very best!

I would rather not go through chemo and radiation. When I see what it does to your body…when I read of the side effects and the possible complications I would much rather throw in the towel right there and say forget it. But yesterday I was reminded that God's plans are truly the best! We may not understand what we are going through, but we can trust God!

As I go forward in this journey since my cancer diagnosis last year, I am taking the time now to remember that I am where I am for a reason. Yesterday I had an appointment for a CT scan to check for cancer again. I went to the appointment knowing that I would be in contact with individuals that I may never see again. Whether they be sitting with me in the waiting room, or whether it is the person that is checking me in to my appointment or the nurses or techs that are going to be involved in my care-God had me there for a reason. One reason is to minister to people that I may never see again! To share the hope that is found in Jesus Christ!

As I said earlier, I would rather not face the possibility of cancer again. I'd rather not have to go through all of the tests, scans and needles (*I hate needles!*). Yet, when I think of the fact that I may never see these people otherwise-I am willing. And not only willing, but I want to! I watched God work yesterday in a couple of instances-1 lady in specific that I want to share with you. Before we arrived to my appointment that day, I stopped at our church to pick up copies of 2 testimony tracts that I had made that share my personal testimony. I figured that as long as I was going to be at the hospital, I was going to make the best out of it by sharing the gospel. When we arrived, I thought that it would be a great opportunity for my husband Joey and our son Caleb to get involved and pass out the tracts while I was getting the CT done. They were happy to. I felt prompted by the Lord to take an extra copy with me when I went to the back. I knew then that there was someone specifically who needed one. Was it a nurse…a tech…another patient? I didn't know. But God did. I should have obeyed that prompting at the time, because by the time I was called to go back, I had forgot to grab a copy. When I got all settled in awaiting the scan I remembered the testimony tract! There was a friendly nurse who I had chatted with while I was being prepped for the scan. It was then I wished I had one of my testimony tracts! After sitting in the back for quite some time, the same nurse sitting at her station asked "is that your boys?" I wasn't sure what she was talking about, but apparently each time the door opened, she could see Joey and Caleb looking back in to see if I was coming out. When I realized what she was talking about, I told her that they could come back with me if they wanted to-so she let them in. They had passed out the testimony tracts all over the hospital-but not all of them! I knew then that God was going to make SURE that specific person was going to get one of these testimony tracts! As the nurse came to my room, she was stunned when she seen Joey. She said it was crazy how similar he looked to her cousin. She said they looked so much like one another. She just stood there looking at Joey; finally she went back to her station. God let me know then that she was the one that needed my testimony and I was to give her a tract. God opened the door WIDE for me to do just that when she came back to my room to show us a picture of her cousin. When she did, I said "here I want to give you this, this is my testimony." She looked at the front, which has a picture of me before I was saved and one after. She looked at it and her eyes widened as she said "yay for the after picture!" I told her to read it when she got time. I told her that Joey and Caleb had been passing them out all over the hospital and she said "well, when I see one I'll be able to say: hey, I know her!" She left, but before she did she thanked me "very much" for the testimony tract. I don't know what was going on in that nurse's life, but God does and He used me and my testimony to reach her. If I were not in the position that I am, I would not have never crossed paths with her. God sees the big picture. He is working behind the scenes of our lives, even when it seems like everything is going wrong.

Divine Appointment

I believe that meeting that nurse was a divine appointment. If I only looked at the fact that I may be facing cancer again, I would have missed the divine appointment-the real reason that I was there in the first place! When the Lord gave me the title of this chapter-"*When life's disappointments reappoint us to God's divine appointments*", He reminded me of the story of the Shunammite women in the book of 2 Kings. She is known as the daughter of Issachar from the city of Shunem. She was a married woman and a woman of wealth. God used this woman, and her husband, to bless the prophet Elisha.

We read about her hospitable nature in 2 Kings 4:8, when the Bible says she fed the prophet Elisha each time that he came through their city. In verse 9-10 she tells her husband: *"Behold now, I perceive that this is an holy man of God, which passes by us continually. Let us make a little chamber, I pray you, on the wall; and let us set for him there a bed, and a table, and a stool, and a candlestick: and it shall be, when he comes to us, that he shall turn in thither."* KJV. This woman of Shunem took great care of the prophet Elisha, and because of the kindness and care she showed toward him, we read later on how God blessed her and her husband with a firstborn son that they had so longed to have. If we read on through the book of 2 Kings, we read more about this Shunammite woman and her family. We read on to find out that the son that God blessed her with died. We read how she layed her son's lifeless body in that little room of Elisha's and ran to find the prophet and bring him back to pray over her son. We read on the find out that she did find Elisha and he did return with her. He did pray over the son and her son was revived! Up and to this point, this woman knew loss. She may have had wealth, but she knew disappointment. She knew what it was like to have a dream in your heart and live a nightmare in reality. Think about it all for a minute. She longed for a child. She watched all of her friends have babies. Each day, she heard the laughter of children playing in the streets of her city, and although she stood in her home that was silent of the pitter-patter of little feet; she finds herself on the outside looking in. Not only did she long to have a child of her own to have and to hold, but she lived in a culture that labeled her as a woman who had sinned because she was "barren". She lived with a broken heart and a label. What amazes me about this woman when I think about her is the fact that her situation, and her feelings about her situation, did not define who she was. Although she felt like she was robbed of the joy of motherhood, she was still giving. Although she may have felt rejected in society, she was still hospitable. She had needs and wishes of her own, but she provided for the needs of someone else. She still held God in high regard as we see her telling her husband that she perceives Elisha to be a holy man of God. She held the Lord in highest esteem as she made a place in her own home for the travelling prophet; carefully planning for Elisha's needs as she had the room fully furnished. It was a special place for the prophet Elisha to stay. The last of her life's story unfolds before us as we read 2 Kings chapter 8. It is in this chapter that we read of God's judgment on Israel because of sin. We read how the prophet Elisha is faithful to return care and kindness to this woman and her family when the prophet comes to them to warn them of the coming drought-a drought that will last seven years! The news must have been bittersweet. They must have been thankful for the warning, but heartbroken because of what it meant. More loss and more disappointment. They had to leave everything behind that they had worked so hard for. They no doubt faced the struggle of their lifetime as they had to decide what they were going to do and where they were going to go. This was no vacation. They were fleeing a drought and one that was expected to last 7 years! 7 years! Let that sink in for a minute. It had to be devastating news. It was life-changing news to say the least. We read that her and her family sojourned in the land of the Philistines for those 7 years. Then we read one of the greatest stories of divine appointment and reappointment that is found in the Old Testament. It is the culmination of everything we have read about her life up and to this point. 2 Kings 8:3-5 KJV says: *"And it came to pass at the seven years' end, that the woman returned out of the land of the Philistines: and she went forth to cry unto the king for her house and for her land. And the king talked with Gehazi the servant of the man of God, saying, Tell me, I pray you, all the great things that Elisha has done. And it came to pass, as he was telling the king how he had restored a dead body to life, that, behold, the woman, whose son he had restored to life, cried to the king for her house and for her land. And Gehazi said, My Lord, O king, this is the woman, and this is her son, whom Elisha restored to life."* CAN I TAKE A MINUTE RIGHT NOW TO PRAISE THE LORD? WOW, WOW WOW!!!!! What a divine appointment! This woman who knew pain and heartache, disappointment and loss, was about to receive the biggest turnaround in her life! Only God could set something up so perfect-so divine! At the very moment that the prophet Elisha's servant is talking to the king about the mighty workings of Elisha, the very one who **received** one of those miracles at his hands comes walking in the room-WITH the son that was brought back to life by Elisha!!! Get ahold of this with me for a minute-God made sure that Gehazi was where he was at the time he was, talking to the one he was-and not just talking to anybody; he was talking to the very one who had the power to do something about her situation! And that's exactly what happened! After the king asked the woman all about it, the Bible says: *"So the king appointed unto her a certain officer, saying, Restore all that was hers, AND all the fruits of the field SINCE THE DAY that she left the land, EVEN UNTIL NOW."* (2 Kings 8:6 KJV)

A disappointment turned into a reappointment

Do you realize that just as the king was the one who had the power to restore this woman's house, her land and the fruit of her land, God is the One who holds all power and He is the One who commands the blessing over us? The king said ***"Restore all that was hers…"*** At this point, it was as if the Shunammite woman had never left her homeland for seven years because the king restored everything that she thought she had lost! That story is a perfect picture of how God commands restoration in our lives! Let me tell you, the Lord is showing me even as I type this to you, that it doesn't matter what you have been through or what you are going through, it doesn't matter what you have forfeited because of your own ignorance or have had stolen from you by the hands of the enemy, GOD WILL RESTORE BACK UNTO YOU AND UNTO ME EVERY SINGLE THING THAT WE HAVE LOST! Every opportunity that you has been taken from you…Every promise that you thought was not coming to pass…Every dream that you gave up on because you thought it had died… God will turn it all around for you! He will bring healing and restoration back into your home…Back to your relationships and back into your finances! He will bring your children back to where they need to be. Pray and believe! Keep trusting in the Lord. Don't ever give up and at just the right time, GOD will command restoration over you and your household! The Shunammite woman had to go through some things, yes she did. But did you notice what the scripture said in the beginning of chapter 8 verse3? It says ***"And it came to pass at the seven years' end, that the woman returned out of the land of the Philistines:"*** It came to pass…at the seven years' end. What "came to pass" at the "seven years'end" is that the drought was over! She and her family were able to return home! What was awaiting her was a divine appointment- scheduled by God himself. She had her miracles in her life, given to her by God through the prophet Elisha, BUT NOW she was going to receive the miracle of restoration and it was given to her this time straight from the hand of GOD! We may not know what God's plan involves for our lives, but I am certain that if we will look past our circumstances, we will be able to see God working in and through our lives, not only to bring restoration to us and to our families, but restoration and hope to those with whom we meet on this journey of life.

CHAPTER 6

WHEN THE UNEXPECTED HAPPENS

There have been times in my life when I thought I had it all figured out; how funny is that? There have been times when I thought I knew what was going on in a particular situation. There have been times when I assumed I knew what God was doing, or going to do, in my life. Lately, it has been one of these specific times for me. I have discovered that it's in these times when I think I have it all figured out that actually- I really don't have a clue!

In chapter 4, *"Willing to Suffer"*, I shared with you how the Lord ministered to me that day standing outside of my house, and gave me the direction that I was seeking regarding taking chemotherapy and radiation treatment. As I shared, I felt the Lord was directing me to proceed with the treatments. It has been a couple of weeks since then, and since I have written, because I have been trying to process everything that has taken place. I have been in a *"where do I go from here"* moment.

The title of this chapter is *"When the unexpected happens"*, and that is because for me, the unexpected did happen to me recently during that latest follow-up appointment. I went to the appointment, eagerly ready for the results of my CT scan and equally ready to proceed with the chemotherapy and radiation. I went into that appointment with a sense of mission: like I was on a God-given assignment. I definitely was, but not like I had figured. God had an assignment alright, and it was a lesson for me!

My husband and I were greeted with the tech who directed us to the exam room. I went through the usual routine: I was weighed, (I thought I had gained but I actually had lost a little, so that was a plus), my blood pressure was checked, (it was very high-no wonder), and the usual questions regarding my health were asked. We then waited patiently for those footsteps and little knock on the door that every patient waits to hear-and it came. The nurse began to review the results of the CT scan. She first informed me that there was no cancer found-**NO CANCER**! Praise the Lord!!! She said that my only ovary was unusually large and had a mass. She said that the Doctor had looked at it, and it did not look cancerous to him. She informed me that the Doctor wants to check it again in six weeks to see if it has gone down and if it has not we will go from there; but she insisted that it would be okay. After our initial relief from the good news we just received, she then asked me: *"Now what have you decided".* I told her that I had decided to go ahead with the chemo and radiation. Her next statement took me by surprise. She said *"About that…the Doctor said it's too late. He said if you were going to do the treatments, you needed to do them no later than 12 weeks post-operative."* I was a little confused at first, but more relieved that it turned out that I **didn't** have to go through the chemotherapy and radiation. I walked out of the office knowing I was going to have to return in six weeks to have the ovary checked, but more importantly that I was not going to have to do the treatments. I was in shock. Not only because I had found out that no cancer had returned, but that I *didn't have to take treatment.* She told me weeks earlier that regardless of the results of the scan, I needed to do the treatments, and now they are saying it's too late? For me, there was a mix of emotions from the office to the parking lot. At first, I was relieved-then I was shocked. Confusion came as I began to think about the last several weeks, and by the time I reached the parking lot-anger set it. My husband was just happy that there was no cancer, and that I didn't have to take the treatments. He took the news for what it was and he was good with that, but not me, I became angry! *"Do they know what I have gone through the last couple of weeks? Don't they realize I am a human? Do they understand the thoughts that I have had? Do they know the agony that I have faced trying to make this decision, and now they tell me "**IT'S TOO LATE**"? That is like a slap in the face!"* I sat reliving the moments in the office as the nurse gave us the news. *"And if she knew it was too late, why didn't she tell me? Why did she* *ask me what I was going to do, have me tell her my answer, and then respond with ITS TOO LATE?"* These are the questions I asked my husband as we sat in the parking lot that day. I couldn't understand it. I thought I had it all figured out. I was going to go into that appointment, and regardless of the results, I was going to tell them that I had decided to go ahead with chemo and radiation. I knew that is what was going to happen because God had given me that direction a week ago. Then my focus was not on what the nurse had just told us, but it was on God. I was very angry at the nurse and the doctor, but now I was confused as I thought about what I had believed to be the plan of God in this situation. I knew that I had God's direction to go forward with the treatments, but now I won't be taking them? What in the world Lord? God spoke to me in the midst of my anger and frustration, and simply said: *"Don't be mad. The doctor and the nurse did not do this, I orchestrated this."* I didn't understand, I thought I had it all figured out-boy was I wrong.

What I began to see that day, is that the unexpected had happened to me. I thought I had it all figured out, but I found out that I obviously didn't have a clue. It was later, as the Lord continued to minister to me that I realized that it was no accident that things happened the way they did, it was the absolute plan of God for me that day. God spoke to me in my anger and told me *"don't be mad."* Regardless of the reasoning behind why the doctor and nurse handled my situation the way that they did, did not matter. God had a plan the whole time, and it was an unexpected plan to me. I expected a lot of different things, but God had other plans than what I had expected. I began to ask the Lord about why He asked me that day if I was willing to suffer for him. Why did I feel Him leading me and preparing me to take treatment if He knew I wasn't going to have to take it? I couldn't understand.

It was in the coming moments and days that God began to show me that what was unexpected to me, was not unexpected by Him. It didn't take God by surprise when the doctor determined that it was too late for me to take the treatments. That decision was not thwarting the plan of God in my life. It was God that orchestrated it! Why? God then reminded me of the story of Abraham and Isaac. Isaac was the promised son. God had promised Isaac to Abraham and Sarah years before he was born. Isaac was a product of a seemingly impossible circumstance. We know that what is impossible with man is not impossible with our God! We know that Abraham and his wife was long past their child-bearing years, but God made the promise of a son. God is faithful, and He was faithful to keep the promise of this son, Isaac. When the timing was perfect, Sarah gave birth to Isaac-just as God had promised. Abraham's future rested in this promised heir. However, there came a day in Abraham's life that the unexpected would happen. In Genesis chapter 22 we read of one of the biggest tests in Abraham's life.

> *Genesis 22:1-2 KJV-"And it came to pass after these things, that God did tempt Abraham, and said unto Him, Abraham: and he said, Behold, here I am, And He said, take now thy son, thine only son Isaac, whom thou lovest, and get thee into the land of Moriah; and offer him there for a burnt offering upon one of the mountains which I will tell thee of."*

Sacrifice my son? But God, you gave Isaac to me! God, you promised Isaac to me and to Sarah! If I am to be the father of many nations and all families of the earth through me will be blessed, how will that be if I sacrifice my only son? Don't you remember God, how you took me outside and had me look into the sky at all of those stars? Don't you remember telling me that my seed would be as the stars of heaven? God, you know I only have this one son, and if I sacrifice him as you say, how will I have seed as many as the stars of heaven? Abraham did not ask any of these questions, but I probably would have. When God instructed him to sacrifice Isaac, he did not try to figure out what God was doing and why. He just trusted God. Hebrews chapter 11:17-19 KJV tells us:

> *"By faith Abraham, when he was tried, offered up Isaac: and he that had received the promises offered up his only begotten son, of whom it was said, That in Isaac shall thy seed be called: Accounting that God was able to raise him up, even from the dead; from whence also he received him in a figure."*

Abraham believed in God to the point that he was willing to sacrifice his only son. He didn't question God, or try to figure out the plan and purpose of God; he simply obeyed. God did not require Abraham to sacrifice his son. God had to put Abraham to the test to see if he truly was willing to do what God asked of him-no matter the cost. God did not want Isaac; He wanted to see that He had Abraham-all of him. Abraham was willing to give God everything-even his only son. The only way to show that Abraham was fully devoted to God was to put Abraham to the test. It was a test that Abraham passed, as we read in Genesis 22:11 KJV:

> *"And the angel of the Lord called unto him out of heaven, and said, Abraham, Abraham, and he said, Here am I. And he said, Lay not thine hand upon the lad, neither do thou any thing unto him: <u>for now I know</u> that thou fearest God, seeing thou hast not withheld thy son, thine only son from me."*

The words *"for now I know"* are what show the finality of Abraham's test. God could have only *asked* Abraham if he would be willing to sacrifice Isaac, but until he actually put action behind his words there would have been no test at all. Abraham did act, and because he was willing to do what God asked, it proved Abraham's faithfulness to God.

As God reminded me of this story, He showed me that they only way to prove that I was willing to suffer for His sake, as He had asked me weeks earlier, was to actually put me in a position where I thought I would have to. By taking chemotherapy and radiation, I was willing to put my own comfort to the side, and go forward with it because I believed it to be what the Lord wanted me to do. I had thought that the Lord wanted me to do it not only to kill any cancer cells that may be in my body, but more importantly because I would be able to minister to those who have had the same experience. I would meet people that I would not otherwise come in contact with, and I would be able to tell them about the love and power of God. Physical suffering not doubt would accompany the treatments. I also knew from the experience I had from surgery and recovery, that it would not only be a physical battle, but a spiritual one as well. I just came out of the toughest physical and spiritual battle in my life back in May, but I was willing to do face it all again because I thought that is what the Lord wanted me to. For his sake, I was willing to suffer. At first, I was so angry that the nurse asked me what I had decided to do after she gave us the results. *If she knew it was too late for me to do treatments, why didn't she just tell me that first? Why did she have to actually **ask me what my decision was** if she already knew the outcome?* The Lord showed me, that was my own *"for now I know"* moment. Just as Abraham journeyed to mount Moriah, laying Isaac upon the wood-his hand raised to slay his only son, I had to put action behind my words, and tell them my answer. God did not require Abraham to slay his only son, and He did not require me to go forward with treatments. Just as God was testing Abraham to see that He had Abraham's full devotion no matter the cost, God tested me to see that He had my full devotion no matter the cost. I said that I was willing to suffer for His sake, like Abraham, my actions proved it.

It has been through this time of testing, that I have learned that just when I think I know exactly what God is doing, I really don't have a clue. I have learned that God is working and God has a purpose and plan in every situation. I learned that it's an even bigger purpose and plan than we can even think or imagine. When life isn't going as you have planned, and you are faced with unexpected circumstances, you can still trust God. In the moments where it feels you have lost your handle in a matter, remember God is in control! God knows what He is doing, even if it is unexpected to you. He still requires your faith and obedience no matter the cost and regardless of what the situation may be.

CHAPTER 7

THE BEAUTY IN OUR BROKENNESS

The beauty in our brokenness, now that's something that will make you think. It is certainly something that made me think when God revealed to me that it would be the title of this very book. Initially, beauty is not what we think of when we hear 'brokenness' and it definitely is not something we see in something that has been broken. We see damaged. We see unusable. We see unsalvageable. We may try to fix that broken toaster, or that stubborn washing machine that has quit working for the umpteenth time, but when our husband breaks out the duct tape, we quickly realize that there are just some things that duct tape *won't* fix. When something breaks, we usually retire that item to the trash can and go buy new. We know the throwing away of broken items is common practice, but what about broken relationships? What about when our own lives feel broken and way beyond repair? Don't we do the same thing then, and just throw it away so to speak? Sure we do. Divorce rates prove it, and so do suicide rates. But nothing and I mean no-thing is beyond God's repair-not a broken relationship-not even a broken life...**my life is living proof**.

The matter of finding beauty in our broken lives is a matter of perspective. It is a realization that even though something is broken, it does not mean that it is of no use. It is not automatically resigned to the junk pile just because it may be chipped or cracked-even shattered. It can still be useful, and even have value. *Our lives* **definitely** have great value, no matter how broken we may be! When searching for the right perspective in our brokenness, the Japanese art called *kintsugi* has been an eye-opening revelation for me. Kintsugi is a Japanese technique that repairs broken pottery with a type of lacquer that is mixed with gold, silver, or platinum. Instead of repairing the piece to **disguise** the brokenness, the repair is done in such a way as to **highlight** the broken pieces. The philosophy is that by highlighting the brokenness in the piece, it makes that piece even more beautiful. Each piece that is restored has its own story and its own one-of-a-kind beauty. Our lives are like that. We don't like our brokenness to show. We do everything we can to hide it. But the truth is, each one of us has been 'broken' in some shape or form. It's when we allow others close enough to see our scars and brokenness that we realize that we are not alone. Like the broken pieces of pottery that is repaired to show the breaks, we all have a story. Our lives are able to shine with a one-of-a-kind beauty when we allow God, the Master Potter to take those pieces and make a beautiful creation. Only God can take the pieces of our shattered lives and make us even more beautiful than before. God is in the business of restoration. God is the One that quite literally makes beauty out of our brokenness.

My "Testimony Tree"

I have been through enough in my life to know that it doesn't matter how broken, how shattered, or how absolutely beyond repair your life may be, God can fix it! God can mend it! God can completely restore it and transform it! My life is living proof! I was reminded of this one day as I was feeling the pain of brokenness in my own life. This time, God used a tree to speak to me; a tree that I now affectionately call my "testimony tree". Here's my recount of the very day that God showed me that there truly is beauty in our brokenness!

The sound of a chainsaw rang out one spring morning as I just sat down with my first cup of coffee. As I glanced out the window, I saw that the tree-trimmers had arrived. Just days before, a storm came through and destroyed the most beautiful tree in our front yard. After the howling winds and torrential downpour the night before, I awakened the next morning to its effects. My favorite shade tree was destroyed! This tree once had the loveliest shape; at one time it stood tall and proud. In the summer it was full of luscious, beautiful leaves. The best part of having this tree was the shade that it provided to a large portion of our front yard. Now after this storm, the majority of this once majestic tree now laid in a sprawling heap over our lawn. The tree trimmers were there to see to it that the tree was removed-or so I thought. After about an hour or so, I heard the truck pull away. I was excited to see how the front lawn looked without the mess of what was left of our once beautiful tree. As I looked out my window in eager anticipation, I beheld the ugliest thing I had ever seen! "What are they doing?" I thought. I wanted the tree cut ALL the way down, leaving no trace of this ugly monstrosity. But now, I was left with the biggest eye-sore ever, a giant stump-and it was right in the front of our house! Every day I had to look at this awful remnant of what once was so beautiful and brought me so much joy. Now that tree brought many other feelings, but joy was not one of them; I absolutely hated it! It wasn't until several months later that this tree became a very big blessing in my life, which I now thankfully call my "testimony tree".

I was in my yard one day and I was feeling very discouraged. I thought about all of the bad things that have happened in my life. As I sat there, it was as if I had a little devil with a pitchfork sitting on my left shoulder whispering all of the memories of days gone by in my ear. I made the mistake that day of entertaining those thoughts and recounting the details of those horrible memories. Sexual abuse for the first 11 years of life= the shame. The guilt. Used. Dirty. Damaged. Ruined. Feelings of worthlessness from a very young age. Feeling Unloved. Unclaimed. Uncared for... Looking for someone/something to fill the emptiness inside= Nothing. No good. Empty. Lonely. Broken. Unworthy. High School drop-out=Failure. Dead-end road. No use. Nothing to offer. Pregnant Teen= Broken dreams. Shame. A disappointment.

Just one word from God can completely change your perspective

Unprepared. Single and struggling teenage mother=Inexperienced. Unprepared. Scared. Unstable. Unqualified. Years following were filled with struggles and brokenness and left me feeling like a failure every day. The guilt. The shame. Unfixable. Damaged. Destroyed. As I recounted all of these terrible memories and more, I realized that I was sitting in a very defeated position-literally. I had first sat down in my chair to enjoy the sunshine, but by the end of me recounting all of these memories, I was sitting in a very slumped over posture. I took notice of it, as I sat up and leaned back into my chair. It was then that I asked God the infamous question: "WHY? Why did all of these things have to happen in my life? I mean, really. Why didn't you stop it all from happening? What was the point of going through all of those horrible things? It was then that God answered me, but not with the answer that I thought. As I looked up from my chair, I looked up at that old ugly tree "stump". Something caught my attention. It was a small sprig of green poking out from a crack in the center of the damaged, dead-looking tree. What in the world was this growing out from this tree? I hadn't noticed it before. As I walked over to the tree to get a closer look at what was growing from it, God began to speak to me. He said *"Just like you thought this tree was the ugliest thing you had ever seen and that it had no purpose anymore and you just wanted rid of it- that is how you view all of the things that have happened in your life. But just like the promise of life springing out of that tree, I am going to bring life out of all of those things that you have been through."* I was shocked! Just moments earlier, I had felt so discouraged and defeated, but now I had the feeling of love and peace, and it filled my soul! When God speaks to you, everything changes!!! Just one word from God can completely change your perspective. God gave me a promise that day that has changed my perspective and my entire life since. God truly has brought beauty out of all my ashes. In every circumstance that seemed hopeless He made a way. When I was in my darkest moments, He was the one who carried me through. In the moments that I was alone and felt no one cared, He showed me that He was with me and that He loved me. Considering everything I have been through, I could have easily become a statistic in so many ways: BUT GOD! Because of God's redeeming power, my life has been restored and transformed completely! I am no longer broken. I have been made whole by the grace of God. Instead of a broken heart and damaged mind, I have joy in my heart and have been given the mind of Christ! I know who I am in Christ and I know whose I am! God has truly brought beauty out of my brokenness!

Many times, especially when we are living in the middle of our brokenness, our perspective is not very clear. Life's challenges can be overwhelming and we can be left with the feeling of hopelessness and a sense of helplessness. When a situation, circumstance or a tragedy leaves us feeling anything but whole, many questions begin to fill our minds: '*Will I ever find "normal" again? How will I ever be able to live again after this?*' What we are really trying to understand is how to be whole again when you are in a state of brokenness. Maybe you are broken in your health; maybe you are literally broke financially. You may be experiencing brokenness in a relationship or a friendship. For you, it may be that an unexpected tragedy has left you shattered beyond words. No matter what your situation is, you're probably filled with many questions, including the "why" question like me. Brokenness in any form leaves us all with questions. Questions like: Is possible for my life to be whole again after it has been shattered beyond repair? I am broken; can God still use me? And just maybe you are wondering, can God take my brokenness and make something out of it? The answer is:

YES, GOD CAN!

There is nothing that God cannot do! He heals the hurting, mends the broken, and brings back to life that which is lifeless. He takes what is shattered and makes it completely whole again. So, yes God can, AND that's what God does! And again, my life is living proof. I am reminded of a wonderful scripture that has given me so much encouragement and hope throughout the years, especially in the times of breaking. It is the story in the book of Jeremiah that tells us of how God is the potter and we are the clay. It is found in Jeremiah chapter 18 verses 1-6 KJV: ***"The word which came to Jeremiah from the Lord saying, Arise, and go down to the potter's house, and there I will cause thee to hear my words. Then I went down to the potter's house, and, behold, he wrought a work on the wheels. And the vessel that he made of clay was marred in the hand of the potter; so he made it again another vessel, as seemed good to the potter to make it. Then the word of the Lord came to me, saying, O house of Israel, cannot I do with you as this potter? saith the Lord. Behold, as the clay is in the potter's hand, so are ye in mine hand, O house of Israel."***

Do you want to know what I get out of this scripture that has brought me the greatest hope in the most discouraging and broken times in my life? It is the fact that no matter what it is that I have *went through, going through* or *will ever* go through, God is working a work through it all. Even in the pain. Even in the sickness. Even in the discouragement. Even in the hopelessness. Even in the tragedies of life. In the brokenness. When I'm stretched to my limits. When I don't think I can go on. When it feels there is no use to keep trying- God is working a work! I may not understand it-many times I don't. I may not have all the answers to my whys-many times I don't. I may not know when things will start looking up. I may not see how God will turn it all around for my good. But I *do* know that I can trust God. I know that God is good. I know that He is my Heavenly Father and He only wants what is best for me. He sees what I can't. He understands what I don't. He is making a vessel of honor out of me and He knows what it takes to make me into the final masterpiece that He is creating. You and I are that work on the wheels. Remember that you are not a finished product. Your situation may have left you feeling like there is no coming back from it. You may feel like it's all over. But remember the story of the potter and the clay. The Lord said that as the potter was working that clay on the wheel that the vessel that the potter was making became *"marred"* in the hand of the potter. That word *"marred"* means that the vessel the potter was making was ruined in his hand. You may feel ruined. Your life may seem ruined, but take heart, because the story did not stop there! The scripture goes on to say *"so he made it again another vessel, as seemed good to the potter to make it."* **So he made it again another vessel….**Your life is not ruined! Your story is not over! God is the potter and you are the clay. He will take every broken piece of your life and make it beautiful. He is the Master Potter. God has done it for me, and He will do the same for you.

I know that every broken situation that I have experienced has helped shape me into the person that I am today. I wouldn't be who I am today had it not been for those experiences. I know that I would not have been able to have written this very book that you now hold in your hands had it not been for all of those experiences. The good, the bad and the ugly. And, I would not be able to tell you that God can and will restore your life-no matter how broken! I have learned by my own experience that there is NOTHING THAT GOD CANNOT DO! God Himself reminded us of this fact when He spoke to Jeremiah again and said: ***"Behold I am the Lord, the God of all flesh: is there anything too hard for me."*** (Jeremiah 32:27 KJV) ABSOLUTELY NOT! There is NOTHING too hard for God! He is ALMIGHTY! That means He is the head of all power-IN HEAVEN AND IN THE EARTH! It is the Lord God Almighty who created the world. It is the Lord God Almighty who spoke and it was so! It is the Lord God Almighty who created the planets, and the galaxies and who hung the stars in space and knows them all by name. (Psalm 147:4). There is no situation God can't change, no sickness God can't heal, no life or relationship that God can't restore, no brokenness God can't bind up, no hurt God can't mend, no person that God can't transform-AND USE FOR HIS GLORY!

You might be reading this, and you may be experiencing what seems to be endless pain, overwhelming challenges and maybe even tragedy has left you in a state of shock and loss. I too have been there. But let me tell you that the ONE THING that has brought me through every single thing in my life is not a "thing" but it is a PERSON. That person is Jesus Christ. Whatever it is you might be facing, call upon the Lord and He will answer you! (Jeremiah 33:3) Trust in the Lord in your circumstance! **He will bring beauty out of your brokenness!**

Me and my great-grandparents
Earl and Eathel Fisher at church

Me at age 2

Me in 1986 on Easter morning

Our wedding day

Our family photo Oct 2016

Savanna playing dress up-red tights and all

Caleb just minutes after birth

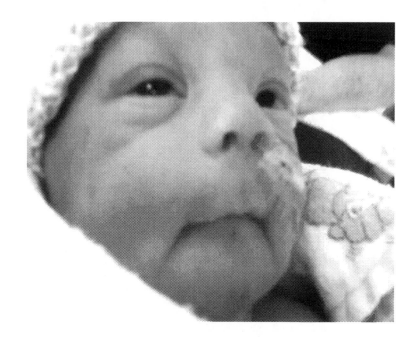

Caleb Lee in the NICU

Holding Caleb for the first time. Oh what a feeling!

Our first grandchild Tavryn James

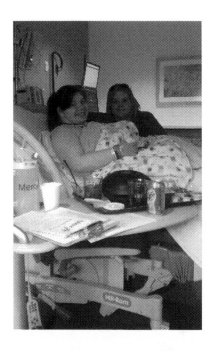

My baby had a baby! Me and Savanna after the birth of Tj

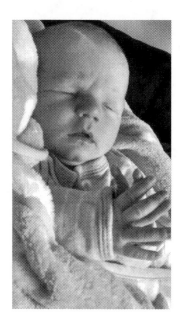

Grandma's prayer partner

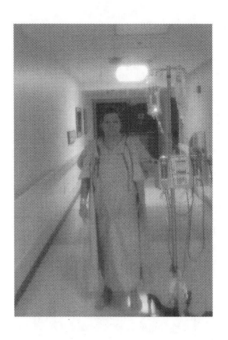

My operation after cervical cancer diagnosis-May 2016

Joey, Caleb and I at the 2016 Relay for Life in Nixa Missouri a few months after my first operation for stage 3 cervical cancer.

Joey and I after my lobectomy. No cancer detected!
God is still a miracle-working God!

My testimony tree standing in all its glory!

CHAPTER 8

THE TRUTH, THE WHOLE TRUTH, AND NOTHING BUT THE TRUTH

It is a consuming passion of mine to give hope to hurting and broken people. To not only *tell* them, but by my own life *show* them that **God can** heal, restore and transform a life, no matter how broken it may be. The Lord revealed to me that in order to see deliverance and healing begin for others, it <u>REQUIRES</u> me to be open and real about my own personal struggles. He showed me the importance of sharing not only the good parts, but the bad *AND* even the ugly parts of my life. Did I just say that? Yes I did, and "open" and "real" will take on a whole new level of meaning for me. Here goes....

Just one of the lessons that I have learned about brokenness is that when you think you have been as broken as broken can possibly be, you find out you were wrong. Circumstances and situations hit you out of nowhere revealing a part of you that has never been touched by true brokenness; and then the Lord reveals that particular part of you and begins the process...

I thought my previous battles had prepared me for what I was about to face. I thought I'd have enough strength and determination to hit the ground running on this one; in many ways I did, except in this *one area*. I began to see what was unfolding. I began to see what was about to be revealed. Uncovered. Something I had kept to myself...hidden for so long. Something that I kept covered up under a "mask" figuratively speaking but also quite literally. The Lord allowed this new situation to arise in order to begin a new process in me. It was a new journey that would leave me completely open and vulnerable. He was taking me to another level, and it *required* me to be vulnerable. Real and Raw. The absolute truth of me. The whole truth and nothing but the truth so help me God. So-Help-Me-God…which was and is my literal prayer! So here I go….

In 2 Corinthians chapter 12, we read of a very real struggle the Apostle Paul was faced with. Paul called it a "thorn in the flesh". The specific circumstance of exactly what this "thorn in the flesh" was has been the topic of debate for many years. Many bible scholars have said that the Apostle had an infirmity in his flesh-a physical illness that he struggled with. Some have said it wasn't a physical illness, but the thorn in his flesh referred to an individual who was against Paul and made themselves an enemy, coming against Paul and bringing slander to his ministry. Whatever the case, one thing we are not left to question is the effect it had on the Apostle Paul. Starting in verse 7 of chapter 12 we read: *"And lest I should be exalted above measure through the abundance of the revelations, there was given to me a thorn in the flesh, the messenger of Satan to buffet me, lest I should be exalted above measure. For this thing I besought the Lord thrice, that it might depart from me. And He said unto me, My grace is sufficient for thee: for my strength is made perfect in weakness."* KJV Here we see Paul's struggle. Whatever this struggle was, it was allowed by God. It was an experience that God allowed in Paul's life to keep him humble, but it was something that Paul prayed three times for God to deliver him from. I know all too well what that feels like-to have a certain struggle that seems to never end. To know that God can heal me if He just speaks the word. To earnestly pray for God to remove it, take it, to heal it, to deliver me from it. But just as He did Paul, God's answer was not one of deliverance *from* my problem, but the strength-*His promised strength* to make it *through it*, in spite of it. And that's when God's strength is truly realized-*in* **our weakness.**

I don't know what the Apostle Paul's thorn in the flesh was, but I sure know what mine is-PCOS! For those who may not know what that it is, it stands for Polycystic Ovary Syndrome. My thorn in the flesh is a physical ailment. I had it for many years before I was diagnosed by a Doctor. I didn't know that it actually had a name; all I knew is that it wreaked havoc on my body and in turn-my life. The symptoms of PCOS began just beneath the surface-hidden and unseen. In my early twenties, my body's chemistry started spiraling out of control. Mood swings, weight gain and irregular periods left me feeling like a mess- daily. Soon the inward symptoms I had been experiencing would make a debut on my outer appearance, driving me further into a confusing tailspin as to what was really happening to my body. Unbalanced hormones were playing ping-pong with my health, and when the first signs of facial hair began to appear, I knew something was really wrong with me. I was a young woman with a very serious problem. At the time that the symptoms started, I didn't know the Lord, so I had nowhere to turn. I didn't understand what was going on with my body, all I knew was I could not let anyone find out about it. The embarrassment from it all kept me locked up in a prison of fear. Fear that someone would find out, as the facial hair was the leading factor in my self-made prison. A prison of isolation that I would protect myself inside of for years to come.

I had struggled with PCOS for about 10 years before I was actually diagnosed with the condition. "You have what we call Polycystic Ovary Syndrome, or PCOS." I finally had a name for all of the madness. The doctor told me of the options that were available, but none of them were a cure-only a temporary "band-aid" for the symptoms. For those who have PCOS there is no cure medically speaking. I was placed on medication that the Doctor said would help with one of my most problematic symptoms- the facial hair, which I found out, also had a name- *hiruism*. Hiruism I thought was such a strange name. I thought such a name was fitting for a woman who grew facial hair-strange. A name that sounded closely related to *hideous*-which is how I felt.

> ✠
> No-one really understands the struggles that come along with PCOS, except for those who have PCOS
> ✠

Facial hair is NOT something that young women are supposed to have. I remember how it made me feel the first time it started making an appearance. I know how I felt then, because it is still how I feel today. I

HATE IT! Waking up every single day having to shave your face is not the best way for a woman to start off her day. There are other treatments for facial hair, such as laser treatment, but those can be very costly. So, my beginning struggles consisted of finding just the right kind of razors to use that wouldn't cause razor burn-further complicating the already so complicated health issue I already had. Even finding the right type of shaving cream that won't wage war with your body's chemistry is something that one struggling with PCOS might encounter. All of this became new territory for me, and it was territory that I had rather not have to tread. I did not sign up for this! No-one really understands the struggles that come along with PCOS, except for those who have PCOS. There are SO MANY factors. The shame and embarrassment alone is something that is a real battle for so many of us who have PCOS.

I learned very early on, that this thorn in my flesh was something I **did not** want to talk about, and it was something that I did not want anyone to know I had. Not even my husband knew I had it. I remember the day that he found out. Being an outdoorsy family, we love being in the great outdoors, enjoying things like swimming and fishing, and we also enjoy camping very much. Early on, I can remember my husband's frustration one day as we were trying to plan our next camping trip. Every single place my husband recommended-I refused. It wasn't because the places he recommended were terrible for camping; actually they were just the opposite. Each one of his ideas were the *ideal* camping location, which was the cause for my husband's frustration, and the puzzled look he had when I rejected every last one of them. The locations were perfect! Forests, mountains and spring-fed waters were brimming with the promise of landing the big catch-one that we could fry up fresh on a hot campfire. The great outdoors were calling our names! The ideal camping destinations, with everything you could ask for-except for one thing. None of the places he recommended had shower amenities. Those amenities can be a little scarce when you are in the camping world. My husband was suggesting the more rugged, wilderness type of places. His idea of camping was to find a wooded, secluded area, far away from any of the modern conveniences we enjoyed at home. But I couldn't do that, *I had PCOS*. I needed somewhere with running water so I could take care of this daily problem that existed in my life-but he had no idea. He didn't understand why I turned down every single place that he suggested. I so very much *wanted* to go to those places, but I just *couldn't*. PCOS can control so many aspects of your life. That was the day I finally told him *why* I couldn't go to any of those places. Between his frustration, my secret struggle and my brokenness over not being able to do something I really wanted to do, the tension was too much-I broke down and in shame and embarrassment told him my struggle. He was shocked, and not in the way I had thought. He was shocked that I had been struggling with this for so long-*alone*. I felt a huge weight lift off my shoulders as he wrapped his arms around me and held me tight. The door to my self-made prison of isolation had been opened, and my hidden struggle had finally seen daylight. Now, my husband and the Lord were the only ones that knew my struggle...until now.

As I mentioned earlier, the Lord had revealed to me that in order to see deliverance and healing begin for *others*, it <u>REQUIRES</u> me to be open and real about *my own* personal struggles. PCOS is something that I have not been open about, and definitely not as open about it as I am right now. I have dealt with the issues that it brings-silently. Unlike the beginning of my PCOS journey, I have a personal relationship with the Lord now. He has helped me through all of the struggles. Like Paul, I have prayed and prayed for the Lord to take this from me, but He hasn't. Yet just like Paul, His grace has been sufficient for me!!! I am convinced that the reason the Lord did not, and *has not* taken this thorn in the flesh from me is so that I might bring hope and help to someone else that may be going through the same thing, or something similar! I still have PCOS. I still have to wake up every single day and deal with the effects it has on my body, but if I can help just one person, my struggles are worth every single bit of what I have had to go through!

The Lord began to show me most recently, that it was time to open up about my struggle with PCOS. In October of 2018, my oncologist was concerned with some symptoms I had been having as it related to the cervical cancer I had in 2016. So because of those concerns, a PET scan was ordered to take a look see and make sure the cancer had not returned. The good news came first in just a few days that there was no cancer detected anywhere where it had been, but the bad news was that thyroid cancer had been detected on the right lobe of my thyroid. There was also concern that it had spread to at least two lymph nodes in my neck, as all of this showed up on the scan. The following weeks were filled with further testing and biopsies and we finally decided on surgery to remove the right side of my thyroid which had the tumor. They were confident that the surgery would take care of everything, and that I wouldn't need any further treatment. My surgery was scheduled for the beginning of November. As I prepared for the thought of surgery, and as I read over the instructions for the surgery prep, I began to realize something bigger than an operation was about to take place. "Houston we have a problem" took on a whole new meaning for me. I started to get the revelation that this surgery would be on my **neck**-the same location that for years has already been dealing with problems of another nature. The doctor assured me the incision would not be very long, and that the scar would fade in time. All I could think of was how that scar was going to draw everyone's attention to my neck. I had tried for years to deflect that attention from that area, now this scar would be like a bright flashing neon arrow saying LOOK AT THIS! I had figured I had done a pretty good job at covering up the 5 o'clock shadow with my careful choice of just the right shade of foundation. Even finding makeup can be a struggle for someone dealing with PCOS. I had found a good makeup regimen that did a satisfactory job through the years of covering up this dreadful situation. If people *had* noticed the 5 o'clock shadow, they didn't comment-for the most part. There were a couple of times where something was mentioned. One time, someone asked me why my neck was bruised. I was as shocked as they were by that question, and it stung me deep down inside. That was always a secret fear of mine-that someone might ask me directly about it. Now, facing surgery, I realized the literal mask that I had been hiding behind was going to be put "in the spotlight" so to speak. After surgery, people would now notice this fresh new cut going across my neck, something I would not be able to cover up. As I read the surgery prep instructions, I was filled with even more dread as realized the next hurdle in trying to keep my struggle a secret. No make-up for the day of surgery! Those of us familiar with surgery prep know the pre-op instructions. Very detailed instructions on the do's and don'ts prior to your operation-things like: no eating or drinking after a certain time the night before, showering with the bacterial soap, and on my surgical prep instructions-no make-up. My heart sank. Not that *cancer again* was not enough, not that I would have to endure the looks, the endless questions and blank stares at my neck, or the potential questions about why my neck is dark, but this too? Like I don't have enough to be concerned about the day of my surgery, *now I have to worry about this*, I thought. No make-up meant my problem would be COMPLETELY UNCOVERED! There would be no way to hide it. What will I say to everyone? Our Pastor and a few others from church were planning on being there for me for support. They are going to see this! What will I say? Those are just some of the thoughts I had about it. I had confided in my daughter a few days before the surgery. In compassion, her response was: *"Mom, just tell them you'll be okay, that they don't have to come to the hospital. They will understand..."* But I just couldn't do that either. I knew I was just going to have to face it. Whatever happened was just going to happen; I had absolutely no control over the situation. At one point, I contemplated on going ahead and wearing just a little foundation anyway, and had it not been for the fear of *that* being discovered and the reason for a possible surgery cancellation, I would have done it. But how in the world would I explain why I wore makeup to my surgery? So I did what I always knew to do, and that was just deal with it. It was what it was. What was going to be was going to be. What they would say they would say-I had no control over any of it. All that I knew was I had to have this surgery, period. Let me tell you what a completely humbling experience that it was! That was the most vulnerable position I have ever been in-in my life. I was completely exposed to the world. I could no longer hide behind the mask. Looking back, I understand why God allowed it. I can see that the entire situation had to happen in order for this very chapter in this book to be written! I would have never opened up about it unless the Lord allowed me to be put in that situation. I dreaded every step in that journey, but I found out in the end, that everything was ok. **I was completely open, uncovered and vulnerable**. No make-up, no mask. That morning, I woke up with Psalm 46 verse 5 on my heart: ***"God is in the midst of her; she shall not be moved: God shall help her, and that right early."*** (KJV) God knew His word is what I needed to hear that morning. I clung to it as I faced the day. Before I had time to get fully awake and start worrying over what lay ahead, God gave me a word-HIS word! God truly helped me that day and *"right early"*. When I arrived at the hospital and was admitted, I wasn't met with peeking glances, or awkward questions. With my bible spread across my bed, opened to Psalm 46, I found myself surrounded by my family, church family and nothing but love.

The days following my surgery were a time of recovery for me, and from far more than just my operation. I was sent home the day of my surgery with a set of instructions on how to properly care for my incision site. It was appropriately titled *"Wound Care"*. Specific instructions were given regarding the incision. One of those instructions was to *'keep the area clean and dry, and open to the air.'* I was to keep the area *uncovered* if I wanted it to heal properly. I learned that the risk for infection was higher if the wound was covered. The Lord began to minister to me regarding this very thing. Through those post-operative instructions, the Lord showed me the necessity of my struggle to be uncovered. In order for proper healing to take place within me, my internal wounds needed to be <u>uncovered and open.</u> The risk of internal damage is greater when it is covered up and hidden. What I thought was protecting me from harm, was actually the breeding ground for a very serious problem, and the Lord was not having that. The Great Physician knew what He was doing. His plan of care for me required each of those painful steps to get me to a full and complete recovery. This journey led me to the place of healing on the ***inside***, a wound that needed healing for a long time.

In order for healing to come, first for ourselves and then for others, we must be open and honest with whatever we are facing. That means you have to get real and stop hiding behind your mask. It takes a level of complete vulnerability, but I promise you that God will not leave you hanging out on a limb by yourself! No matter what struggle or thorn in the flesh you are dealing with, remember that God's grace is truly sufficient for you-His grace ***is enough***! Remember the Apostle Paul's prayer? Like Paul, God may not remove that problem or situation- your 'thorn in the flesh' but He will give you His grace for every day. Remember God's response to Paul-it's our answer in these times as well. His grace was sufficient for Paul, and it is still sufficient for us! **It is in your weaknesses, that you discover His strength like never before.** So, as one who has walked the path of struggles and hard times, and walked the road of recovery to complete restoration, I want to assure you right now that there is truly light at the end of the tunnel. Allow yourself to be open and real. Keep putting one foot in front of the other, and keep your hand in His-He WILL see you through to the other side!

CHAPTER 9

NO PAIN, NO GAIN

Maybe you have heard it said: "If it doesn't cost you something, it isn't worth anything" and I for one wholeheartedly agree. The Lord Jesus Christ is our *ultimate example* of what it means to pay the price. Our redemption came at a price. He knows the ultimate cost to redeem mankind back to God, for He was the one who paid the debt of sin, which was death. Romans 6:23 KJV: ***"For the wages of sin is death; but the gift of God is eternal life through Jesus Christ our Lord."*** <u>**The wages of sin is death'.**</u> I am so thankful there are two parts to this verse because it doesn't stop there. First, we learn the price for sin, which is death. But then, (and thank God for this), But <u>**the gift of God is eternal life through Jesus Christ our Lord.**</u> Two very powerful statements, joined by a very blessed word: BUT. There is a price for sin, and Jesus paid it all IN FULL! Because Jesus suffered for our sins through the death on the cross, paying the penalty of our sins, we are able to be saved and inherit eternal life! We are the ones who have **gained** everything-all because of Jesus and **His** sacrifice! Jesus knows all about 'no pain, no gain', but it is very hard for us to grasp this concept in our walk with the Lord.

One individual that really encourages me is King David. God was with David and did many mighty things in and through his life. Scripture doesn't only show us the good things about David, such as the fact that he was a man after God's own heart, but it includes every part-even the things you wouldn't want anyone to ever know about. David's victories were chronicled, and so were his failures. After David sinned with Bathsheba, the man after Gods own heart was the same man who confessed to the prophet Nathan, *'I have sinned against the Lord'*- David's sin had found him out. David's life is laid out before us-his life is a literal open book and I for one am so glad that it is! It gives me hope when I read of the grace of God that strengthened David and wrought victories, and the forgiveness for his failures by that same grace. To know that God is no respecter of persons gives me hope when I'm facing a failure or a victory of my own. David's pain is my gain!

Maybe it was curiosity, or maybe it was a time in his life that he was feeling insecure, but nevertheless we read of a different time when David failed and what it cost him. We read in 2 Samuel chapter 24 that David ordered Joab to number the people of Israel and Judah-something the Lord instructed David not to do. As the story unfolds, we read the judgment of God that came because of David's disobedience when the pestilence came upon the land, and seventy thousand men died in 3 days' time. David was quick to recognize his sin and equally quick to repent. He was instructed by the prophet Gad to ***"rear an altar unto the Lord in the threshingfloor of Araunah the Jebusite."*** *(2 Samuel 24:18 KJV)* After being instructed by the prophet of the Lord, David quickly moved to obey. As David and his men approached Araunah, he was greeted with great respect and honor, as the scripture tells us that ***"Araunah went out and bowed himself before the king on his face upon the ground."*** *(2 Samuel 24:20)* As David explains that the purpose of his coming was to buy the threshingfloor and build an altar to the Lord, Araunah offered David everything that he needed to do just that-free of charge. What we see next is the heart that David had for the Lord. It was at this point that David could have said, *'Great! I came to purchase the land from you but this is even better, I'll take it!'* but David knew that it really wasn't a true sacrifice unless it cost him something. When Araunah offered everything for free, David said with a full determination ***"Nay, but I will surely buy it of thee at a price: neither will I offer burnt offerings unto the Lord my God of that which doth cost me nothing."*** *(2 Samuel 24:24)* David insisted on purchasing the threshingfloor and the oxen for fifty shekels of silver. Because of David's repentant heart and true sacrifice, the judgment of the Lord was stayed and the remnant of Israel was spared. David knew that if he was to give the Lord his God a true offering, it was going to cost him. It wasn't about the money, but the true offering was David's devotion to the Lord-even when an "easier" way presented itself.

I want to be used of God. Let me rephrase that...I really, sincerely and with all my heart want to be used of God; I really, really, **REALLY** do! As a matter of fact, that has been my #1 consuming desire of my life since I met Jesus! And the one thing that I am learning about that is that <u>if I really, really, **REALLY** want to be used of God, it is going to cost me something.</u> My desire to be used of God fully, and completely as He sees fit, is going to REQUIRE that I experience some things that don't always feel so good. It is going to require the complete dying of self, so that the Lord can be exalted. As John the Baptist said: ***"He must increase, but I must decrease."*** *(John 3:30) Wait* a minute, *I must DECREASE????* "Dying to self" doesn't sound near as bad as it feels. Dying to self is one of the hardest, and I mean HARDEST things we can ever learn to do as a human being! By nature, we want what **we** want! "Self" craves comfort. "Self" likes being pampered and coddled. "Self" feels good when it is attended to and all of its wants, wishes and desires have been fulfilled. "Self" doesn't like to be stretched or to be challenged, put to the test and God forbid- broken. But oh, the process of dying to self, that is a painful process! It begins at the moment of conversion, and it is a life-long process that we must continue if we really want to be used of God.

One of the most important lessons that I have learned about dying to self came during a very challenging time in my life. It was a time when everything around me felt like it was falling apart. Finances were not great and the bills were piling up. Between my husband's work schedule and my college classes, the time we spent together was few and far between. During this time, we were having a difficult time connecting with our daughter, and our schedules were not helping her in the least. And in the midst of our chaos, was the adversary- and he wasn't letting up. I felt as if I was smack dab center stage, and every where I turned and looked it was a test, a trial or struggle in some way. I remember it was during this time in my life that I learned many valuable lessons. It took me being under pressure and feeling like I might break under the load of it all to realize I was in the best possible position- **if** I truly wanted to be used of God like I said I did. It was at this time in my life that the Lord spoke something so simple, yet so profound and life-changing. I remember that day like it was yesterday. I was standing in my kitchen cooking dinner. It was a Wednesday night, and I was scheduled to minister that evening at our church. The Lord gave me a message about victory and how He gave King Jehoshaphat victory over the enemy, but it took the king being in a situation he couldn't handle to realize he needed to look up to the Lord for help. There could have been no greater message for the Lord to give me that night-not only to preach for the people, but for myself! Even though the Lord was trying to minister to me, I was completely oblivious to what the Lord was trying to show me; all I could focus on was everything that was going on in my life. Me and the Lord were having a real heart-to-heart that day in my kitchen. 'How in the world can I minister to other people when I need ministered to myself', I thought. I have ministered during some really difficult times in my life, but this is one time that I just can't do it. So, with that, I decided to call our Pastor and let him know that I would not be able to preach. I was prepared to hear him encourage me, as he always did, to 'trust the Lord' and 'press through' and preach any way, that 'the enemy wanted to shut me up' and how I just needed to 'stand my ground and show him a thing or two', but I didn't hear any of that this time. After I told him that I "just can't", he just simply said, "ok"-but oh the Lord was NOT letting me off the hook that easy! Even when I told the Pastor "I can't" the Lord said "yes you can". Even when I hung up the phone, the Lord kept encouraging me. As I said, I was in my kitchen cooking dinner, but it might as well of been a wrestling ring because there was a fight happening right there in my kitchen, and I was wrestling with the Lord. "How can I *possibly* minister to anyone right now"… the Lord reminded me of the message He had already given me. "But *I* am so broken right now"…the Lord reminded me that He would strengthen and help me. Clearly, I was losing the fight with the Lord, so I felt like I had to make a final stand-the one last ditch effort to get the Lord to see it my way, and let me have my way. Oh how foolish I can be. So with all the strength I could muster I finally said: "Lord, you know! If anyone knows, you do! I have been able to press through every other time, but this time **I** *CAN'T!*" That's when I was taught a valuable lesson. God's simple, yet profound and life-changing response was: *"Good. Now we're finally going to get somewhere."* At that very moment the wrestling match was over and God had won. It was then that I *realized* **I can't…** I *really* can't-and I never can. But HE CAN! When we have exhausted all human ability and resources, we realize that all we really needed to do is look up to the One-the only One who *is* able. God is the One who gives us strength; His help is available to us the moment we ask. He will empower us to do the work He has set before us. It is not in and of ourselves that we accomplish anything and sometimes it takes a little (or a whole lot) of pain and pressure to realize it, and to break our will- so that His will can be done…that is when God can do the greatest work. Let us be willing to lay down our very lives for the Lord. Let us live a life that says *not my will but thy will be done.* What we will gain-and what others will gain, will be worth it all.

CHAPTER 10

IT DIDN'T COME TO STAY
IT CAME TO PASS

Six years *to the day.* It was March 29, 2010 that I found myself at this exact same hospital, but for a very different reason. Then I was in pre-term labor. I was seven months pregnant and my water had broken at home. I went to a hospital that I had originally planned on delivering at, but due to the fact that they didn't have the necessary accommodations to handle a premature birth, I was transported by ambulance to another local hospital- the very one I found myself at on this very day-six years later: March 29, 2016.

My husband and I were patiently waiting in the room for nurses to take me back to have my first PET scan. Earlier that day, I had just been diagnosed with cervical cancer. The doctor believed they had caught it early. They needed to get a scan of my body to determine the size and location of the cancer, and to see if it had spread to any other areas in my body. I was immediately scheduled to have a PET scan. As the doctor made the arrangements, she sent me directly over to the hospital that day. Never having been through anything like this, I was a little anxious to say the least. There came a fear; it was a fear of the unknown. I had no idea what I was about to go through. **I did have a very real sense that I was at the beginning of a new journey in my life.** The moment you hear the news *"you have cancer"* your life as you know it changes. So many thoughts start swirling around in your head. So many questions; accompanied by all of the "hows" and "what ifs". A cancer diagnosis is definitely a life changing experience like none other. This day we were taking the first step in that new journey with cancer.

Waiting is something that not many of us like to do-especially when there are so many unknowns. As I sat awaiting the PET scan that day, I had so many questions and plenty of time to ponder them. I wondered just how far the cancer had spread. Did they really catch it early? What if it has spread throughout my body and *if it did*, how long will I live? Having family members that have been through the cancer journey, including my mother, I knew about Chemo and Radiation Therapy. I was well aware of its affects. Will *I* need chemo or radiation-or both? These are just some of the things I pondered upon that day as I waited for my name to be called. In between my waiting and my questions, came a revelation from God. I had no idea the connection that God was about to make for me. As I sat there in that waiting room unsure of what I was about to face, I began to fidget with my hospital bracelet. I swirled it around and around my wrist, much like the questions in my mind. I stopped swirling it around my wrist long enough to see the date-*March 29, 2016*. March 29. I knew something was strangely familiar with that date, but why? I began to think about it and that's when the Lord brought it back to my remembrance. This was the day I was here when my water broke when I was pregnant with my son. It was *at this very hospital, six years ago to this very day*! The memories of that day six years ago came flooding back in my mind. Like this day, I was very unsure what I was about to face. The fear of the unknown was very real. I was only seven months along; it was too early to give birth. The baby was not ready to be born yet; he had a whole two months to grow and develop. I was scared for his life. "*Will he be ok?*" was the main concern out of the many concerns that I had that day. I did not know what would happen, or how things was going to turn out, but I knew the One who did and I held onto God with everything that I had in me. I was taken from the ambulance to the Labor and Delivery floor and admitted into the hospital that night. I was met with a team of doctors who evaluated and assessed my situation, and met with me and my husband to let us know what was going on and what the plan was going forward. They explained that since my water had broken, I was going to have the baby, but their goal was to keep him in the womb for as long as they could. They explained to me that they would accomplish this through a combination of a certain type of medicine and bed rest. It was at this point I was certain that I was not going anywhere and that I was there to stay. I found myself at the beginning of a journey and there was no turning back. They told me that the longest they would be able to keep me from delivery was approximately one week. During this time, they would give me medicine that would speed up the development of the baby's lungs, which would greatly improve his chances of survival. The idea that there might be a chance your unborn child *won't survive* is a feeling I can't put into words. Only mothers and fathers that have been faced with that possibility know what it feels like. I was ordered on strict bed rest, and the doctors left me with a lot to think about that night. For the next six days, I stayed in my hospital bed, awaiting the arrival of our little baby boy. I spent those days praying for God to make him strong so that he would be able to survive. I prayed for God to use the medicine to speed up his development; so that his little underdeveloped lungs would be developed enough to be able to live outside the protection of my womb. I remember the night before I gave birth. It was crazy to me, because I woke up every hour on the hour exactly, and it wasn't because the nurses were coming into my room to give me medicine, or to check my vitals. It was so strange. By the time 9 a.m. rolled around, (which was the usual time I woke up each morning), I knew something was different about that day. I remember telling my husband that I was going to have our son that day. I just knew it. As the morning wore on, contractions began slowly. By noon, they were pretty consistent, and by early afternoon I was moved from my regular room into the delivery suite. It was finally show time-or so I thought. While in the delivery room my contractions became more and more inconsistent. By about 3 pm I was moved out of the delivery suite into a room next to it. There, I was being closely monitored and should I go back into active labor, they could quickly get me back to the delivery suite. After a couple of hours that is exactly what happened. After 24 hours of active labor, I gave birth to a 4 pound 4 ounce 15 and ¾ long precious baby boy. The neonatal intensive care doctors and nurses were on standby, and they were quite surprised about his size. For his gestational age, they expected him to be about half that weight. That was just one of the early answers to prayer! The moment that our son was born, my first question was *"is he okay?"* I didn't hear him cry. Those were some of the scariest minutes-minutes that seemed like an eternity. After a few moments, I heard the sweetest little cry I had ever heard! It was such a tiny cry, and I knew just by the sound of it he must have been so little. The doctors quickly evaluated his little body and instead of placing him in my arms, he was placed in an incubator and quickly taken to the Neonatal Intensive Care Unit for further evaluation. Mother and baby went separate directions-he went to the NIC Unit and I went back to my regular room. None of what I had just experienced was what I had planned. In my mind, I was going to carry him to full-term and deliver a healthy bouncing baby boy. According to *my* plan, I should be holding my son right now. As they wheeled me out of the delivery room, I realized that was not to be. Although I was experiencing something very different than what I had planned and *expected* to happen, I knew beyond a shadow of a doubt that God was with us and He knew what He was doing. I knew that God had a plan and all of this-even every scary part of this, was a part of His plan.

Although I knew God was with us and had a plan, I felt so helpless as a parent during this time. Watching them wheel him away to the NICU in that incubator was the beginning of the helpless feeling I felt after he was born. I remember before they took me to my room, they wheeled my hospital bed into the NICU so I could see him. The first time I was able to get a good look at my son, he had wires all over his body and he was hooked to so many machines. He was so tiny! He had tubes going in his nostrils, an IV in his little arm and monitors all over his body. I wanted so much to be able to do something and to change it all for him. I wanted so much to pick him up from that little isolet and hold him in my arms but I couldn't. His little body was not used to life outside the womb, and nurses quickly explained to me that any stimulation would not be good on his fragile system. I was heartbroken. It was at this time that God spoke to my heart and He told me that although I could not hold my little baby boy, **HE** was holding Caleb in the palm of His hand. I knew those were the best hands that he could possibly be in and that gave me some peace then and in the days and weeks to come.

The following six week journey continued to be filled with God's favor and answered prayer. I quickly realized that God had been guiding this situation all along. From the very first day when my water broke at home to the days and weeks following his birth, I realized God had a specially designed plan for every step of our journey. It was during this time, that I learned what it meant to fully lean on God. I found out that when you have nothing and no-one else to help you-God is there, and He is the greatest help there is! I learned to fully trust in God. I couldn't protect my baby from coming into the world unprepared. He was premature. I could not stop him from being born. I couldn't keep him within the protection of my womb, but it was during this time that I learned that we were under a different kind of protection-*God's divine protection.*

Now, on this day, March 29, 2016- I was asking a similar question that I had asked six year previous. Instead of asking *"is **he** ok"* the question I was now asking was: *"will **I** be ok?"* As I looked at the date March 29, I began to realize God's perfect sovereignty. It was no coincidence that I found myself sitting in the same hospital that was I was sitting at previously, six years to the day. Now instead of having a baby, I was diagnosed with cancer. It was then, when God began to show me that everything was going to be ok. God gave me a word that day, as I looked down at that hospital bracelet. He spoke to me and told me that just as He brought me through that journey six years ago, He was going to be with me and bring me through this new journey with cancer. As I found myself on the first step of this new journey, I found out that God was right there with me. God gave me an assurance that no matter what path was ahead for me, no matter what I had to go through, and no matter what I had to face, I was going to be ok and <u>He was going to bring me through it all</u>.

Early in the journey when I had our son, I found God had special and unique ways to encourage us. He did so in so many ways, some of which were ways that if you weren't careful, you might even miss it. From the special doctor and nurse that God divinely assigned to me to the way he provided every single need right down to the smallest of things; I experienced God's "winks" and they accompanied us all along the way. One of those ways that God encouraged me was through a picture that hung on the wall in the hallway near the NICU. I passed it every time I went to see Caleb, which was continuous. I had passed by the picture several times not paying much attention to it, until one day I stopped long enough to read it and I am so glad that I did. It was a verse from Ecclesiastes chapter 3; it was verse 1. It read: ***"To every thing there is a***

season, and a time to every purpose under the heaven..." *KJV* This picture hanging in this hallway became a constant reminder for me that *this too shall pass* It reminded me that I would not always be visiting Caleb in the NICU; there would come a day that we would bring him home. It is so important to remember when you're in the midst of a difficult situation that it will pass! When you're in the middle of it all, it can seem like nothing will ever change. There are days that feel the situation will never change, and at times you can feel very hopeless-but with God there is always hope! If we pay close attention, He has placed encouragement all around us-His word being the greatest encouragement of all. As I stopped that day to read what was on the picture in that hospital hallway, the scripture read, *'to every thing there is a season'*. There is something we all know about seasons and that is **they change**. Winter, spring, summer and fall are seasons. Each season has an appointed duration of time. Each season is necessary for a healthy working environment. There are certain things that are accomplished within the duration of a season. For example, during the winter season as the snow falls to the ground, nutrients are being added into the soil. Nitrogen is one of the elements that is absorbed into the ground when snow melts. Nitrogen is *essential* to plant growth. If it doesn't snow, the ground does not get the nitrogen that it needs. In the wintertime God prepares for the plants in springtime, with this essential element. Not everyone fully appreciates the snow, especially individuals such as myself. I absolutely love the scenery when it snows. I absolutely love watching my children and grandbaby play in it. But I *absolutely don't like* to drive in it. But all the while, in the midst of the snow covered roads, God is doing something far greater than initially meets the eye. There is a greater purpose being accomplished when it snows, and just like that- a greater purpose is being accomplished when we find our lives in a season of difficulties and hardships. Remember that no pain comes without a purpose. Just as that picture hanging in the hallway with Ecclesiastes chapter three verse one was there to be a great encouragement for me in my time of need, pay close attention to the things that God has placed for encouragement along the "roads" and "hallways" of your life. Just as simple as that verse on a picture in the hospital hallway, or the date on my hospital bracelet that I could have easily overlooked-be careful not to miss God's encouragements He has placed all around **you**! These are the very things that God gives us to hold on to that brings us great encouragement while we travel from one season of life to the next.

Whatever difficulty you may be faced with, let Ecclesiastes chapter 3 verse one be a reminder for you. Remember that there is a greater PURPOSE in your pain, a PLAN in your hardship, and TRIUMPH in every trial and tragedy in your life. Whatever "it" is, hold on and remember that *it didn't come to <u>stay</u>, it came to <u>pass!</u>*

CHAPTER 11

THE GOOD, THE BAD AND THE UGLY

We have heard it said that before there's a message there has to be a mess, before there's a testimony there has to be a test, and before there's a triumph, there has to be a trial. That statement is so true! If you were to ask me if I want my life to be a living testimony, I would not hesitate to tell you *absolutely!* What about being triumphant? Well, again- *absolutely.* What about being a Jesus lovin' child of God with a message to share with the world? I would say with all certainty-*ABSOLUTELY!* But then what if you told that me that before I could be that living testimony, I would have to go through testing? What if you said that before I could be triumphant, I would have trials to face? If I wanted the message, I must first have a mess. Would I still be eager to answer with the same fervor and passion as before? Good question. <u>The thing is, *we all* want the testimony, the triumph and the message-we just don't want to go through what it takes to obtain those things; *not really.*</u> But in order to have those things, we must experience what it takes to have them-the ups **and** the downs, the health **and** the sickness, riches **and** poverty-all of it: the good, the bad **and** the ugly!

There is no other time in my life that I have been closer and more connected to God than when I have went through a test, a trial, and when everything in my life seemed to be a mess. I am able to say that now, but when I found myself in the midst of those things it didn't *feel* like that **at all**; actually quite the opposite. But what I didn't know then that I do know now is what those situations in life produce in the end. I have been through times in my life when it felt like I was going through a trial all alone. Situations in my life have come along like a gigantic storm out of nowhere with winds and rains that tested me to the point I felt like I would break. Those storms of life left what seemed like nothing but a mess of devastation and loss. It was in those moments, that I wondered where the Lord was in the midst of it all. Desert experiences left me feeling like the dry bones that were described in the book of Ezekiel-*very dry*. And just like God asked Ezekiel, I asked God- *"Can these dry bones live?"* Although, the tests were difficult, although the trials sometime came what seemed like one after another, and although I stood in the midst of many messes that the storms of life left behind, *it* was in these lessons of life that I discovered God to be God. It was in these experiences that I learned that truly He my sustainer, my deliverer, my shield and my rock-unlike any other time in my life. It wasn't 'in spite of' but it was *because of* these experiences-the good, the bad and the ugly ones that I gained a better perspective, a perspective that helped me to overcome the adversities and to keep going forward.

Written within the pages of the New Testament is one of the greatest examples we have of someone who trusted God no matter what opposition or victories he experienced, and that is the Apostle Paul. Paul knew adversity. Imprisonment, beatings, and opposition are some of the things the Apostle encountered in his pursuit to fulfill God's will. Paul wrote to the Corinthian church and told them about some of the things he had experienced along the way. *"Are they the ministers of Christ? (I speak as a fool) I am more; in labours more abundant, in stripes above measure, in prisons more frequent, in deaths oft. Of the Jews five times received I forty stripes save one. Thrice I was beaten with rods, once I was stoned, thrice I suffered shipwreck, a night and a day I have been in the deep; In journeyings often, in perils of waters, in perils of robbers, in perils by mine own countrymen, in perils by the heathen, in perils in the city, in perils in the wilderness, in perils in the sea, in perils among false brethren; In weariness and painfulness, in watchings often, in hunger and thirst, in fastings often, in cold and nakedness. Beside those things that are without, that which cometh upon me daily, the care of all the churches."* (2 Corinthians 11:23-28 KJV) When I am in the midst of adversity and I feel like I have had about all I can take, I am encouraged by the testimony of Apostle Paul. Throughout scripture, he shared many of his life experiences, and this scripture in 2 Corinthians has been one of the most encouraging to me. I have experienced adversity, yes. I have experienced rejection and persecution, yes. I have even experienced some physical pain and suffering along the way, but none of the things I have encountered can be compared to the things the Apostle Paul did and yet he kept moving forward-*and with a passion!* The Apostle Paul's testimony has been one of greatest encouragements to me to trust God in my journey no matter what kind of adversities I face.

The Apostle Paul knew what he was gaining despite his trials and adversities, as well as his victories and triumphs-something that we all too often forget-*contentment.* I believe contentment was one of the leading attributes that made Paul a successful overcomer and a humble conqueror. I believe it was one of the main things that sustained him in the face of adversity, and kept him humble during times of prosperity. Contentment is an inner sense of peace; a peace that comes from God. It is a peace knowing that God is in control no matter what is happening to us, or around us. This kind of contentment is not something that we instantaneously possess. Paul explained how he came to possess his contentment in Philippians 4:11-14 KJV: *"Not that I respect in want: <u>for I have learned</u> in whatsoever state I am, therewith to be content. I know how to be abased, and I know how to abound: every where and in all things I am instructed both to be full and to be hungry, both to abound and to suffer need. I can do all things through Christ which strengtheneth me."* Contentment was not instantaneous for Paul, <u>it was something that he had to learn</u>. Paul's contentment came as he persevered and kept forging ahead in the good times, and especially in the bad.

Life is a great teacher. Have you ever heard of "the school of hard-knocks?" Many of us have attended this very school; we are familiar with the courses it has to offer. Life has a way of giving us lessons-all kinds of lessons all along the way. Some of the greatest lessons in our life are taught by adversity. We become a stronger version of ourselves having come through adversity and we are better because of it. Everything Paul experienced-the good, the bad and the ugly life experiences served to be the very situations that God used to bring about this great contentment in Paul's life. The struggles and the victories were the lessons that taught him how to overcome and be victorious through every one of his situations. Because of his contentment, whatever situation Paul found himself in, he had that God given peace that all things were going to work out for his good-and they most certainly did! Many of the things Paul experienced in and of themselves was not very good, but each circumstance served as a schoolmaster that taught very valuable lessons in the end.

Paul was able to continue in the work God assigned him because he had contentment. One of the greatest testimonies to me about the Apostles life is that according to his circumstances, and what could have been the most discouraging times of his own life, he was an encouragement to others. During a time in his life when he was under severe persecution, to the point of imprisonment awaiting execution-Paul wrote a letter of encouragement to Timothy. When Paul penned the second letter to Timothy, not only was he in prison awaiting his execution, but he was experiencing disappointment from many different situations. First, Paul was disappointed with the believers in Asia who turned away from him. (2 Timothy 1:15) As if that wasn't enough, Paul was also faced with more disappointment when Demas deserted him and the mission *"having loved this present world."* (2 Timothy 4:10 KJV) There is no other heartbreak like what you experience when a friend or a family member turns from serving the Lord and goes back to the ways of the world. Paul had invested his love and time into Demas, discipling him to be fellow laborer in the gospel and a mighty force for the Kingdom of God. Imagine the discouragement Paul felt when Demas chose the world. Following all of these hardships and struggles of disappointment, Paul eventually found himself deserted by all, with the exception of one-the Lord. (2 Timothy 4:16) He had many opportunities to get discouraged, throw in the towel and quit, but we find that Paul did the exact opposite. Paul became an encourager to others. The problems and situations that he faced did not dampen his fervor to fulfill his purpose, it became like the fuel that made his passion burn hotter. Many of us are tempted to focus on the situation we are in, instead of the One who will help us and who will bring us through whatever we are facing. Because Paul had learned to be content in whatever situation he was in, he was able to see to the brighter side of things. In 2 Corinthians chapter 4 we read of Paul's brighter side perspective as we read his words: *"We are troubled on every side, yet not distressed; perplexed, but not in despair; persecuted, but not forsaken; cast down, but not destroyed..."*(KJV)Paul was able to find the good in every bad situation he faced. He had been through enough to know God was not going to fail him. (2 Cor. 1:8-10 KJV) God had provided for his every need. (Phil.4:19) He sustained Paul, and when the going got tough, Paul got going. He didn't let adversity stop him, and he didn't let the victories sideline him. At the end of Paul's life, he wrote his last letter of encouragement and instruction to young Timothy. The aged Apostle Paul was able to confidently say: *"For I am now ready to be offered, and the time of my departure is at hand. I have fought a good fight, I have finished my course, I have kept the faith. Henceforth there is laid up for me a crown of righteousness, which the Lord, the righteous judge, shall give me at that day: and not to me only, but unto all them also that love his appearing."* *(2 Timothy 4:6-8 KJV)* With contentment in his heart, Paul was assured of his final victory in the end. I believe it was that same assurance that kept his eyes on *"the mark for the prize of the high calling of God in Christ Jesus."*(Philippians 3:14KJV) As you travel through this journey called life, may you keep our focus in check and make sure to keep our eyes on that prize.

CHAPTER 12

THE BLACK MARK

I have found that the greatest question we can ask God during the hardest times in our lives is not the one the majority of us are asking. When we are faced with adversity of any kind, naturally, we pray and ask God to change the situation. But I believe the first question we should ask, and the first prayer we should pray is not 'Lord, *will you please change this situation?'*, but 'Lord, *will you please change me so that I may see what it is you are trying to show me and teach me through this situation?'* I have been through enough to know now that God uses the good, the bad and the ugly situations in our lives not to break us, but to make us. God is concerned more about our character than He is our comfort. You will never grow while you remain in your comfort zone. Growth is what the Lord wants in all of us. Growing takes time. Have you ever prayed over a situation, and the situation did not change right away. It probably wasn't the situation that needed to change, but the individual, and maybe that individual was you. It takes situations in life that test us, and trials that pressure us-sometimes to the point of breaking to understand God is doing a work <u>in us</u>. He is not only interested in changing the situation for us, but more importantly, His interest is changing us into His likeness in the process. The tests, trials and even messes of our lives are many times the vehicles in which God accomplishes His will in our lives.

Growing up, there were many t.v. shows my mother would try to get us interested in watching with her. One of those shows was *The Animal Kingdom*. Inevitably, no matter how uninterested we were, she would always manage to capture our attention right about the time when there was a real action scene taking place; you know the one-hungry lion stalks its' prey. The majority of my memories tells me that prey was usually a young tender deer. Mom certainly had our attention then, or better yet, *The Animal Kingdom* had our attention as our eyes were glued to the t.v.-hoping the baby deer would somehow escape the clutches of that mean hungry lion. Our hearts raced at the height of the climactic chase, and more often than not, the lion was the victor. Our pleas to the baby deer to 'run, run, run!' or to the lion 'no, no, no!' were to no avail. And so with that, we were done. It didn't matter what happened next. We were on to the next thing, ready to watch something more exciting and appealing-like He-man or Superman. At least then, we were certain there would be a victorious ending, and who don't like those?

Out of all the shows my mom tried to get us to enjoy to no avail, there was one person she liked to watch that we *actually* enjoyed too-the painter Bob Ross. Known by many for his hair, or of his soft-spoken tone-Bob Ross is remembered by most for his stunning picturesque paintings. We loved watching Bob Ross growing up. He had a knack for capturing our attention from the start. I suppose the one thing that grabbed our attention at the very beginning was his soft spoken tone of voice as he painted-the hair was just a bonus. All of his 'happy little trees' made us giggle and other things he would say such as '*we don't make mistakes, just happy little accidents*' were just some of the things that kept us smiling and glued to his show-'*The Joy of Painting*'. It wasn't until my adulthood that God gave me a revelation regarding Bob Ross and his paintings; a revelation that went far deeper than just the visibly beautiful painted landscapes and scenery.

The black mark

The brush types were specific-depending on what effect he was trying to create. The color choices and the mixture of colors were made with such an exact precision, that only a true master painter would know how perfectly they would blend together to make such a beautiful scene. But nothing could ever prepare me for that one brush stroke with the most striking color attached. The big black mark.

I don't remember a time watching Bob Ross paint, when I wasn't completely mesmerized. Many times, I would catch myself with my mouth gaping wide open, as I watched him turn a completely blank canvas into a complete masterpiece! The final masterpiece took time to complete, but it all started with those first brushes of paint. He always started with a picture in mind, and so with a clear picture of what he wanted to create, he began the process of making the picture in his mind a reality on the canvas. Isn't that like God? God is not only your Heavenly Father, but He is the Creator. He has a "picture" in mind so to speak of what He wants your life to be. Like the blank canvas of Bob Ross, God started making and shaping you into who and what He wanted you to be in your mother's womb. As Psalm 139 verses 13-16 says: *"For you created my inmost being; you knit me together in my mother's womb. I praise you because I am fearfully and wonderfully made; your works are wonderful, I know that full well. My frame was not hidden from you when I was made in the secret place, when I was woven together in the depths of the earth. Your eyes saw my unformed body; all the days ordained for me were written in Your book before one of them came to be." (NIV)* God truly knows what He is doing. He knows every brush and brush stroke, as well as every color and color combination it takes to make the beautiful masterpiece that He is creating, and that masterpiece is you!

There was no doubt as you watched Bob Ross paint, that he knew what he was doing. His skill with paint and brush strokes created some of the most awesome details in his paintings. There was only one technique he used that made me question if he really knew what he was doing, and that was the big black mark. After watching him go from a completely blank canvas to actual scenery that seemed to magically unfold with each stroke, he would then dip his brush into the most unexpected color of all-black. That's when I went from watching a true master artist to wondering if he had actually lost his mind! Down he would go with one long stroke of his brush-a big black mark straight down what was becoming a very beautiful painting! I remember watching intently up and to this point and as I watched him paint that insanely black mark down his picture, I would gasp with all exasperation-thinking he had absolutely and utterly destroyed his work of art! Now was the time you would think of turning the channel, convinced nothing good was going to come out of the painting after that. But just the opposite happened; it made me wonder all the more what was going to become of this once picturesque scene. What will ever become of that black mark? Will it actually turn out to be something good? Does he really know what he is doing?

We all know that life can sometimes be difficult. We can be going along just fine and then all of a sudden-the unexpected happens. Something like a curve ball out of left field when you weren't looking. Now you're standing there, or maybe *fallen down there*, knocked for a loop. Totally oblivious, here it came-a phone call…a Dr's report…an unexpected meeting, called in to the office by your boss…a lay-off…an unsatisfied spouse who has 'fallen out of love' with you…a troubled child who has run away from home. Whatever the 'curve ball' was, it left you in shock. You felt completely blind-sided. Clueless. Reeling. Unsure. Unsettled and maybe PANICKED is a better word for how it left you feeling. Life as you know it has suddenly changed. You find yourself in unfamiliar territory and it feels you are all alone. You wonder *'what happened?' HOW did it happen?* Where do you go from here, and where and when do you start? I am speaking from experience here, and you may be able to relate. Many times in our lives, unexpected events that take us by surprise can feel just like that big black mark down the middle of that painting. We may ask God: *"what are you doing?"* Your life may look and feel like it's totally and utterly ruined now, and you will never recover from its effects. If you are feeling this way, then it's YOU I want to encourage!

> Whether God authored it or allowed it, you can be sure that God is working that situation for your good!

Bob Ross the painter knew what he was doing, and GOD knows even better what He is doing! Whether God authored it or allowed it, you can be sure that God is working that situation for your good! The situation in and of itself may not be good at all, but God will make sure that good comes out of it! Romans 8:28 KJV Paul said: ***"And we know that all things work together for the good to them that love God, to them who are the called according to his purpose."*** Did you catch what he said? ALL THINGS. That includes whatever it is you have been hit with. There is no problem, no situation, no sickness, no tragedy, no unexpected trouble or trial that took God by surprise and one that He will not work together for the GOOD. There has not been one single thing in my life that I defined as bad, which God did not end up working together for the good. Not one. But my life is not the only life that God has done that in. There are many accounts in Scripture of people who faced bad situations, but God turned those situations around for the good. In the Old Testament I think of people like Esther and Job, the Shunamite woman and the children of Israel. Esther lived in a time of great persecution of her people. There was a call for execution of the Jews. It was signed, sealed and delivered by the king. What could they do? There was a death sentence upon their heads. Not a good outlook! But God used Esther, who by God's divine will became queen. God raised Esther up for 'such a time as this' and in the end, saved her people the Jews and granted them protection from all of their enemies! God worked it all together for the good. We've all heard about the patience of Job, and heard many people describe someone of 'having the patience of Job' but no-one really knows what that meant and felt like for Job himself. What we can gather from the account of his life is that it wasn't always a bed of roses for Job. He loved God. He walked in Gods ways. Yet, we see that Job lost all of his possessions, all of his material gain in one day. Not only did he lose all material wealth, but Job lost what was nearest and dearest to his heart also-his children...every single one of them. To show the integrity of this man Job, and a lesson for all of us, is what his response was to his curve ball out of left field. Actually, Job got hit with more like a cannon ball that day than a baseball, but nonetheless, it left him stunned to say the least. As shocking as all of that terrible news of loss had to have been, Job's reaction was not one that many people would have had. The bible says that after receiving the news that he had lost everything he owned as well as all of his children- seven sons and three daughters to be exact, that Job: ***"arose, and rent his mantle, and shaved his head, and fell down upon the ground, and worshipped. And said, Naked came I out of my mother's womb, and naked shall I return thither: the Lord gave, and the Lord hath taken away; blessed be the name of the Lord."*** (Job 1:20-21 KJV)Verse 22 goes on to say: ***"In all this Job sinned not, nor charged God foolishly."*** Worship was Jobs response! Job knew it that moment something that takes the rest of us awhile to grasp. Job knew that even in the midst of his suffering and loss, God was still God, and God was still good. And He was, and He is- even for you! We see that suffering and loss wasn't the end of Jobs story! Actually, the phrase 'saving the best for last' is exactly what Job experienced! God truly worked all things together for the good. At the end of Jobs life, we read in chapter 42 verse 12 (KJV): *"So the Lord* **blessed the latter end of Job more than his beginning:** *for he had fourteen thousand sheep, and six thousand camels, and a thousand yoke of oxen, and a thousand she asses. He had also seven sons and three daughters."* God restored everything that Job had lost, except for now Job had DOUBLE of what he had before! Whatever it is that you have suffered and lost, let Jobs testimony encourage you and your life! Our God is the God of Job! He truly knows how to give you beauty for the ashes, and double for your trouble!

In chapter 5 I spoke about the Shunnamite woman and how her story is one of great encouragement and inspiration. So if need be, you can go back and refresh your memory on her story of redemption, and how God turned her trial into triumph. But let me take a moment right here to share with you encouragement from the account of Gods people-the children of Israel. There are so many stories in the Old Testament from Genesis to Malachi of how God turned seemingly impossible situations into powerful stories of redemption and restoration. After all, God is the One who makes a way where there seems to be no way; and this is an account of how he did that very thing for the children of Israel! What a rebellious bunch they were, and many a time, God had to bring correction upon them. Because they were his children, and because he knew what was best, God hand selected people, places and things to be the catalyst to get them where He wanted them to be. In this account, they were in Egypt, under the rule of Pharaoh and his taskmasters. They had been in Egypt for over 400 years, working as slaves. Through scripture we conclude their lives were spent in anguish and bitterness because of their situation. God's chosen people were slaves! They were tasked with rigorous work day in and day out. To say they were treated poorly and unfairly would be an understatement. Then the Bible says: *"And it came to pass in process of time, that the king of Egypt died; and the children of Israel sighed by reason of the bondage, and they cried, and their cry came up unto God by reason of the bondage. And God heard their groaning, and God remembered his covenant with Abraham, with Isaac, and with Jacob. And God looked upon the children of Israel, and God had respect unto them."*(Exodus 2:23-25KJV) It was at this point in their lives, when surely they were feeling like they were at their wit's end that God sent them a deliverer! Moses was the man that God chose for the job. And in spite of a rough start, Moses obeyed the Lord and went unto them in their mess and distress, and led them out of Egyptian bondage! The big black mark that they had been experiencing as slaves was finally turning into a beautiful picture of redemption. What once stood out as a never-ending mark of slavery and bondage, God turned into the most picturesque turnarounds of freedom, abundance and provision. God once again worked all things together for the good. After the unheeded warnings from God to Pharaoh through Moses, judgment from God began to fall in the form of the plagues. By the tenth plague when death was pronounced upon all the Egyptian firstborn, the Egyptians practically begged them to leave! The very ones who had ruled over them for over 400 years were now paying them to get out of their land! The scriptures tell us that their enemies the Egyptians gave them their own silver, gold and even clothes! So not only did they *beg* them to leave, but they *paid* them to leave! What a turnaround! To better understand how God really turned their situation around for their good in the end was summed up in verse 36: *"And the Lord gave the people favour in the sight of the Egyptians, so that they lent unto them such things as they required. And they spoiled the Egyptians."* (KJV) God truly worked mightily in their mess and in the end, gave them an astronomical blessing and used their enemies to do it!

The blessing of freedom, abundance and provision did not happen overnight for the children of Israel. It took time. They were slaves for over 400 years! It was no surprise to God either. He told Abraham all about his descendents time in Egyptian bondage approximately 430 years before it even took place! God even told Abraham about their deliverance from slavery, and how they would leave Egypt blessed! (See Genesis 15:13-14). God sees what we can't and understands what we don't. We are able to see only in hindsight the purposes in our pain and the blessings that are added to our lives in and through the processes we have to go through.

What I couldn't see or understand as Bob Ross painted that big black mark down the middle of his beautiful picture was that it didn't ruin the painting at all, it was needed in order to complete the beautiful masterpiece that he had in mind all along! He never stopped at just painting a big black mark-that was only the beginning. As I would continue to watch him begin to work with other colors and brushes, little by little I could begin to see an object begin to form. In the *'process of time'* what once was an ugly mark that looked like the ruination of the entire painting, a big beautiful tree emerged and became an essential element and focal point of the entire masterpiece that Bob Ross had in his mind long before it was a finished product on canvas. The picture would have been incomplete without it. And so it is in our lives. You are God's masterpiece. He has something beautiful in mind for your life! So what is the black mark in your life that is threatening to ruin everything that is good? Remember that whatever it is, God is the Master Creator. He doesn't make mistakes. He knows what He is doing. He will take what looks like the ruination of your life and do a work in it and through it that will only be for your absolute good in the end. If you need more encouragement, read chapter 11 of Hebrews! It tells of men and women throughout scripture who really went through some terrible stuff! But God used every situation for their good and His glory. So in your time of trouble, trust the Master in the process. Remember it hasn't taken Him by surprise. He is still in control. He is still God and He knows what He is doing! And as Bob Ross would always do when he put his signature on every one of his paintings, God will put his mark on your life so that nothing or no-one else will be able to get the glory for it all but Him!

CHAPTER 13

THE PROCESS OF CHANGE

There is one thing in life that many people are uncomfortable with and that is change. If I were completely honest, I would say that I have fit into this category myself many different times throughout my life. Change is so difficult for some that they downright fight against it- yet it is an inevitable part of all of our lives. Changes are taking place in the world all around us every single day. One thing is for certain, and that is that we cannot stop the process of change. Not only is it inevitable, but change is necessary!

The older I get, the more I appreciate and even welcome change. I have learned that if you're *not* growing and changing, you're decaying! Change is good, and change is a healthy part of our lives, our relationship with the Lord, as well as the world around us. There are very few things that have taught me more about change than my favorite time of year-spring. Anyone who knows me knows that I LOVE springtime. Where I live, the first signs that spring is around the corner is the arrival of the sound of the spring peepers. I get so excited when I hear the first chirps from these tiny frogs. These spring peepers seem to usher in everything else that I love about spring. Trees begin to bud and blossom, flowers begin to bloom and the grass comes to life once again-changing into a beautiful landscape of green. I guess I love springtime most of all because of the life that comes forth.

Like spring, there are seasons in our lives that seem to be bursting with newness and change, and it's these seasons that we feel are the most rewarding and exciting! Yet, just as it is with all seasons in the natural, our spiritual seasons *change*. Then we begin to experience the times and seasons in our lives when it feels like nothing at all is happening. If you are in one of those seasons right now, I want you to take courage because you may very well be in one of the most important and productive times in your life!

Underground work must be done first before the above ground work can be seen. Before there is a flower, there is a seed. Before there is a mighty oak tree there is a little acorn. We must understand there is a process-it's a process of change. You can't see the seed or the acorn because it's underneath the soil, but just because you don't see it doesn't mean that nothing is happening; no, on the contrary-something magnificent is taking place! And so it is in our lives. God has a perfect design for our lives, and so He begins the process in us. Many times, we see the immediate results of God's handiwork in our lives, and other times, we don't see the results of His work right away so we might wonder if He is still present and working in our lives. But remember God is working even when we don't see it yet. Right now there may only be seeds, but don't underestimate the power and potential of a seed. That planted seed, although unseen, is undergoing a transformation beneath the surface. With the right temperatures, sunlight and water, that seed will begin to sprout out of the ground. With even more time, it will grow stronger and higher and will eventually start bearing the fruit.

PREPARATION TIME

Springtime is a time for the gardening season. Mid March is when my husband and I start planning our garden. After deciding what kinds of vegetables we want to grow in the upcoming season, we determine how much garden space we will need and with that, the tiller is put to use and we start preparing the ground. God has taught me so many spiritual lessons just by naturally tending a garden. I have learned that God has 'set and appointed times'-such as when we are supposed to plant or sow certain plants or seeds, 'due seasons'-such as the times of harvesting but some of the most important lessons God has taught me are regarding our spiritual times of preparation. Just as we have to prepare the ground in our garden in order to receive the seed, likewise, there is a preparation time in all of our lives spiritually speaking.

There is a process to our preparation and it involves the process of time.

Many instances we read in the Bible: *"and it came to pass in the process of time."* We live in a fast-paced, drive-thru fast food kind of world, and if we are not careful, that is the kind of expectations we have about our spiritual progress. But God's ways are not our ways. Much of what God does in our lives requires time and preparation, especially as it concerns our spiritual preparation. We want the blessings right now, we don't like to wait. Many times we feel like waiting is wasting, but nothing could be further from the truth! In God's preparation time, waiting is not wasting-in the waiting He is working! As God is taking time to prepare you, you can be sure no time is wasted. He is using every moment working in you and on you-preparing you for the place He has for you.

TRAINING GROUNDS

In his early life, God had David in a process of preparation. I've often wondered about how David felt as he was in his preparation time. The youngest of 8, David's beginnings were in the fields taking care of his father's sheep-not a very respectable job in that day and time. Day in and day out David had the responsibility of shepherding his father's flock. There must have been days of loneliness, out there in the fields with no other human interaction-just the bleating of sheep. But David was a faithful shepherd, and although we don't know exactly how he must have felt in those early days, one thing we do know is that God divinely orchestrated David's life and the shepherd fields were the training grounds that prepared David for a greater purpose-more than he could have ever imagined at the time!

FROM SHEPHERD TO KING

We read of the thrilling conquests of David, such as his early victory over the giant enemy Goliath, or about how David brought back the ark of the covenant and restored it to its rightful place among the people of God, but one of the most encouraging scriptures to me regarding the life of David is one that is found before we read of anything that David ever did. It is a conversation between God and Samuel. It's just one scripture-1 Samuel 16:1. It reads: ***And the Lord said unto Samuel, How long wilt*** *thou mourn for Saul, seeing I have rejected him from reigning over Israel? Fill thine horn with oil, and go, I will send thee to Jesse the Bethlehemite: for I have provided me a king among his sons." (KJV)* While David was in the field with the sheep, God was orchestrating a plan that was about to change David's destiny! While David fulfilled his duties faithfully shepherding his father's sheep, God was about to promote him to a position high above his present occupation as a keeper of the sheep!

To me, the most astounding and encouraging statements of God to Samuel in 1 Samuel 16:1 is the last one He makes in that verse: *"for I have provided me **a king** among his sons."* (KJV) God provided a king! **When everyone else just saw a shepherd boy-God saw a KING!** David had yet to be called from the field, he had yet to be hand-picked and anointed by Samuel, but God saw a KING all along! The fields in which David led and cared for his father's sheep were David's training grounds, the very place God had been preparing him for the destiny He had for him all along!

Psalm 78: 70-72: *"He chose David also His servant, and took him from the sheepfolds: From following ewes great with young He brought him to feed Jacob his people, and Israel His inheritance. So he fed them according to the integrity of his heart; and guided them by the skillfulness of his hands." (KJV)*

No matter where you find yourself today, be encouraged in knowing that God is using every season of your life as the process in which He is preparing you for the destiny He has planned for you! You may be like David, faithfully serving right where you are-yet unseen and disregarded by all of those closest to you. You may feel totally insignificant, but just like David, God sees your future destiny-the world may see just a shepherd, but God sees a KING!

CHAPTER 14

PREGNANT WITH A PROMISE

I have heard it said that when God makes a promise there is also a process. First, there's the <u>promise</u> then there is <u>perspiration</u> and finally the <u>possession</u>. We see this in the life of Abraham. God first gave Abraham and Sara a *promise* of a son. But before they held Isaac in their arms, which was the *possession* of the promise, there was a time of *perspiration*-or in other words, there was a process in between. For Abraham and Sara, this in-between perspiration time was 25 years! We would much rather skip the process and go straight to the possession, especially when we hear someone's process lasted 25 years! But God knows when we're ready, and although the possession of our promise may not take 25 years, still we cannot bypass the necessary process by which we obtain our promises!

PREGNANT WITH A PROMISE

One day while pondering the promises of God that He has made to me, the Lord began to give me an analogy that I would like to share with you. Here is what I noted in my journal that day as the Lord gave it to me:

"Obtaining the promises of God is much like having a baby. The promise is there, just like the baby is in the belly. You are pregnant. You can't see the baby yet-but you know it's there. You feel it. It's moving, kicking, growing. God's promises: you know He has something for you. You may not have obtained the promise yet, but you know it is coming-you have claimed it's yours by faith. God sends you little reminders all along the way, encouraging you that you are

in deed, carrying a promise! Certain things begin to take place, preparing you to give birth. In other words, things begin to take place in our lives as God is preparing us to receive His promise. One of the first things that begin to happen is the baby gets into POSITION. (Normal birthing position is head down). God gets us into position too! He arranges and aligns us-putting us where we need to be. Next the mother's body begins to PREPARE for birth. Braxton Hicks contractions start, indicating that the body is preparing for the actual birth contractions. God gets us into position, and then begins the work of PREPARING us: teaching, training, pruning, cultivating, correcting, shaping and molding us. The 9 months in the womb is also a preparation time: baby is forming and growing. You do not want to have the baby prematurely! When the baby has not had enough preparation time, it is not ready for life outside of the womb. Having a baby too early is not a good thing; it's not time yet. We don't want to rush God's preparation time either. We risk losing everything if we do. Now there is a time for the PROMISE. There is nothing that can stop it when a baby is ready to be born! The baby is in POSITION, the body has PREPARED itself to give birth as well as the 9 months of preparation time within the womb for the baby, and now it's time to see this PROMISE of life that's been growing and kicking within the womb. Real Contractions kick in, and at just the right moment, the body gives birth to the baby! Nothing can stop God's promises from coming to pass in your life!

I had my son 2 months too early, so I know the complications that come from having a baby before the appointed time. I know the importance of the preparation time, and that it is something that you don't want to rush. But anticipation is something that makes it very difficult to wait for a promise! I want what God has promised me NOW! It wasn't until God gave me the pregnant with a promise analogy that I definitely see the correlation, and I don't want to skip the necessary and crucial processes that precede the promises of God.

It's hard to see the necessity of our waiting period, but when it comes to God's promises, or God's work in our lives, there are critical things happening. It's during this period of our lives that we must trust that God knows what He is doing. He works according to His timetable and He knows precisely the right time to deliver on His promises to us!

Philippians 1:6 says: ***"Being confident of this very thing, that He*** *which hath begun a good work in you will perform it until the day of Jesus Christ:" (KJV)*

Paul is saying here that God is the One who begun the good work in you, and God is the One who will finish it! Do you believe this? Do you believe that if God said it, it is so? Abraham believed what God had promised him, and although it was 25 years before he held his promise in his arms, God did what He said He would do. You may have been waiting in frustration over the pace of your progress or because of the yet to be fulfilled promises that God has made you. But you can fully believe that if God said it, it will come to pass! Remember the 25 year wait for Abraham and Sarah, and yet-they are not the only ones that through faith and patience received their promises! Joseph waited 13 years, and Moses waited 40 years, but while they waited, God was doing a work and in the end, their promises were well worth the wait!

THE WOUNDED BUTTERFLY

I heard a story once that reminded me of the times in my life when I tried to help God out. It was about a man who tried to help out a butterfly, but inadvertently caused damage to it and the butterfly was never able to fly. One day while outside this man watched a butterfly emerging from its cocoon. As he spent several minutes of watching this butterfly struggle to get out of its cocoon, the man thought he would help it out. He took a pair of scissors, and opened the end of the cocoon up-releasing the struggling butterfly. But instead of spreading its wings and flying away, it just flopped around on the ground and never was able to fly. What this man did not realize in his intention to help the butterfly was that the struggle to come out of the restricted cocoon was necessary in order that the fluid in the butterflies wings could be squeezed out-enabling it to fly. Because the struggle was bypassed, the purposes for the struggle were not accomplished and the butterfly was never able to realize its full potential.

Realize your full potential

In the seasons, processes and changes of our lives, there are lessons to be learned and growing to do in each of them. If we try to rush through them, or try to bypass them altogether we can inadvertently miss the significance of each stage and the lessons we must learn in each of them. In turn, our growth will be stunted and our full potential will not be realized. No matter what stage you're in right now, be patient. If you are struggling, stop and ask the Lord to help you learn what it is that you need to learn right now. Realize that wherever you're at and whatever you are experiencing right now, it is only temporary. You will come through this season with a new level of understanding and strength. Like the newly emerged butterfly, you will be opened up to a whole new perspective and you will be prepared to soar!

<u>Don't forget to enjoy the journey!</u>

Remember when you were a kid; you couldn't wait until you were old enough to drive. Once you were old enough to drive, you couldn't wait until you were an official "adult". Then once you actually became an adult and had children of your own, you found yourself giving them the advice you yourself heard time and time again: *Don't rush it! Enjoy being a kid!* If we are not careful, we can be so focused on the destination that we forget to enjoy the journey-LIFE IS SHORT, so let's enjoy the journey!

"PBPGIFWMY"

I didn't know much at the age of about 5, but I was pretty certain I had never seen a word that looked like this one. It was during the 1980's and my great-grandma owned a pin-on button with the big bold letters: **PBPGIFWMY** printed on the front. I remember asking her what it meant, but there was no way for my young, inexperienced self to fully understand what those letters meant then, but I do now. For those who may not know or remember, PBPGIFWMY was a popular acronym in the 1970s and 80s that stands for "Please Be Patient God Isn't Finished With Me Yet". T-shirts, Stickers and Buttons with PBPGIFWMY were all popular ways to remind us all that we are all a work in progress! And so it is today; each one of us are a work in progress! God is actively molding, shaping and making us more and more into His likeness. And that is my whole hearts' desire-not for others to see me, but that they would be able to see HIM!

This book has certainly been a journey. Within the pages of this book and within every line, God is the One who has given me the inspiration and the words. He is the true Author of this book. I have been more vulnerable in this book than at any other time and in it, I have shared with you some of my deepest inner thoughts, struggles and victories in hopes of making a positive difference in your life. It is my prayer that this book was a blessing in your life! I pray that in sharing with you my personal journey you were able to find strength, hope and courage for whatever you are facing and wherever you are at in your life! I pray that this book brought you hope if you were hopeless. I pray that it stirred up your faith to believe in the power of God. I pray that it helped to bring you to the place where your joy has been restored. It is my prayer that these words have given you a new perspective on the struggles, trials and even tragedies that you have faced or may be facing in your life right now. I pray this book helps you to open up and be real so that you can heal, and as the title of this book suggests, I sincerely pray that your eyes were opened to see the beauty in your brokenness and that above all else, that you realize and are assured that there truly is VICTORY IN JESUS CHRIST!!!!!!!!!

LOVE, RAGAN

Printed in the United States
By Bookmasters